Statistics in action

Statistics in action

Student text and unit guide

The School Mathematics Project

CAMBRIDGE
UNIVERSITY PRESS

Main authors   Chris Belsom
                          Stan Dolan
                          Ron Haydock
                          Paul Roder
                          Jane Southern
                          Nigel Walkey

Team leader   Chris Belsom

Project director   Stan Dolan

The authors would like to give special thanks to Ann White for her help in preparing this book for publication.

Cartoons by Paul Holland

Published by the Press Syndicate of the University of Cambridge
The Pitt Building, Trumpington Street, Cambridge CB2 1RP
40 West 20th Street, New York, NY 10011-4211, USA
10 Stamford Road, Oakleigh, Victoria 3166, Australia

First published 1992

Produced by 16-19 Mathematics, Southampton

Printed in Great Britain by Scotprint Ltd., Musselburgh.

ISBN 0 521 42644 8

Contents

Items in *italics* refer to resources not included in this text.

Introduction to the unit

Students should have met concepts covered in *The Normal distribution* before this unit is attempted.

This unit has been written to facilitate 'supported self study'.

*   All solutions and commentaries are in this text.

*   A special tutorial sheet can be used to focus discussion at a final tutorial on the work of each chapter.

Chapter 1

The ideas of significant testing are developed with reference to the binomial and Normal distributions. Particular concepts which are covered include null and alternative hypotheses, one-tail and two-tail tests, significance level, critical region and the two types of error. The final section covers the applications of these ideas to population proportions and opinion polls.

Chapter 2

This chapter concentrates on one sample tests and confidence intervals for population means. For large samples, the Normal distribution can be used. For small samples with unknown σ, the t-distribution can be used providing the parent population can be assumed to be Normally distributed. The t-test is also used to test for a difference using a sample of matched pairs.

Chapter 3

If X and Y are independent Normally distributed variables, then $X - Y$ is also Normally distributed. This result allows the methods of Chapter 2 to be extended to problems concerned with comparisons between two populations means. In contrast to examples where the matched pairs t-test can be applied, independence of the two samples is essential for the application of ideas developed in this chapter.

As in Chapter 2, a distinction has to be made between cases where the population variances are known and those where the variances must be estimated from the samples. For small samples with unknown variance, the t-test can be applied providing a common variance is assumed. The pooled variance estimator is introduced and applied in two sample t-tests.

Chapter 4

For the hypothesis tests covered in the first three chapters, it is necessary either to assume that the population distribution is known or that the sample size is sufficiently large that the Central Limit Theorem can be applied.

This chapter concentrates on two tests, the sign test and the Wilcoxon signed-rank test, which are called non-parametric tests and which do not require any knowledge of the distribution of the parent population. Both tests can be used to find the median of an unknown distribution.

Chapter 5

This chapter introduces the analysis of data concerned with the relationship between two variables. Scatter plots are used to introduce the concept of correlation and this leads to the definitions of covariance and the product moment correlation coefficient.

The idea of 'line of best fit' is developed intuitively. The mathematical derivation of the equation of the line is given in the Appendix. Similarly, the derivation of Spearman's rank correlation coefficient forms extension material, although all students are expected to know how to apply this coefficient to data for which rankings are appropriate.

1 Hypothesis testing

1.1 Making a decision

A teacher has a set of loaded dice which are biased in such a way that the probability of one of these dice showing a six is $\frac{1}{4}$. The loaded dice have become mixed up with a set of ordinary dice so she hands out all the dice to her students and asks them to throw each die sixty times. If a die shows a six on fourteen or more occasions she decides it must be 'loaded'. Otherwise it is classified as 'fair'. The students are then asked to discuss this method of sorting the dice.

 TASKSHEET 1 – *The binomial distribution*

(a) What is the probability that a die is classified as 'loaded' when in fact it is 'fair'?

(b) What is the probability that a die is classified as 'fair' when in fact it is 'loaded'?

(c) Do you think the teacher should change her threshold for rejecting a die as 'fair' from fourteen to

(i) thirteen (ii) fifteen (iii) some other value?

Justify your answer.

(d) Suppose a die showed a six on just two occasions. How would you interpret such a result?

1.2 The null hypothesis

In the example discussed in the previous section, if you start on the assumption that a die is 'fair', then this is called the **null hypothesis**. The **alternative hypothesis** is that the die is 'loaded'.

The conventional shorthand for expressing these hypotheses is

$$H_0 : p = \frac{1}{6} \quad \text{(The null hypothesis)}$$

$$H_1 : p = \frac{1}{4} \quad \text{(The alternative hypothesis)}$$

In this case, you could put a specific value on the alternative hypothesis. This is not always possible.

Suppose a student arranges a number of glasses on a table to test whether a friend can tell the difference between 'diet' cola and 'ordinary' cola. (Each glass is filled at random with either 'diet' or 'ordinary' cola.) He asks his friend, who claims to be able to taste the difference, to taste each in turn and identify what is in each glass.

> State whether you think the null and alternative hypotheses for this experiment should be
>
> $$H_0 : p = \frac{1}{2} \qquad\qquad H_0 : p = \frac{1}{2}$$
> $$\text{OR}$$
> $$H_1 : p > \frac{1}{2} \qquad\qquad H_1 : p \neq \frac{1}{2}$$
>
> where p is the probability that she makes a correct identification. Justify your answer.

A hypothesis is an assumption about the population from which the data has been sampled.

The *null hypothesis* (H_0) is the assumption against which the data is initially compared.

If, after comparison, the null hypothesis appears unlikely, it is rejected in favour of the *alternative hypothesis* (H_1).

1.3   Making the wrong decision

A farmer knows from experience that the yield he obtains from a particular type of tomato plant is Normally distributed with a mean of 6.2 kg and standard deviation 1.8 kg. A friend claims to be able to increase the yield of a plant by talking to it. They decide to put this claim to the test. A plant is selected at random and the farmer's friend talks to it for at least half an hour each day during its growing season.

If μ is the yield in kg of a tomato plant which has received the treatment, then the null and alternative hypotheses are

$H_0 : \mu = 6.2$
$H_1 : \mu > 6.2$

The farmer says that he will be convinced if the plant's yield 'X'exceeds 10 kg. His friend disagrees and feels that the farmer should accept the alternative hypothesis if the plant yields more than 9 kg.

> **Rejecting H_0 when in fact it is the correct hypothesis is called a *type I error*.**
>
> **Accepting H_0 when in fact H_1 is the correct hypothesis is called a *type II error*.**

$H_0 : X \sim N(6.2, 1.8^2)$ $H_1 : X \sim N(\mu, 1.8^2)$

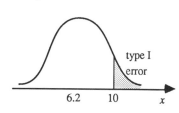   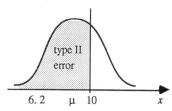

(a)   **Calculate the probability of a type I error if H_0 is rejected for $X > 10$.**

(b)   **Explain why it is not possible to calculate the probability of a type II error.**

(c)   **What would be the probability of a type I error if H_0 is rejected for $X > 9$?**

(d)   **If it is decided to reject H_0 for $X > 9$ rather than $X > 10$, will the probability of a type II error increase or decrease?**

(e)   **The farmer and his friend agree that a probability of 5% for a type I error is reasonable. For what x is $P(X > x) = 0.05$?**

1.4   Level of significance

The cornerstone of English law is that a person is assumed innocent until proved guilty. Similarly, a null hypothesis is accepted until there is sufficient evidence to 'prove' it false.

A null hypothesis is rejected in favour of an alternative hypothesis when the observed data (the evidence) fall into a **critical region.** However, there is always a chance of rejecting a null hypothesis when in fact it is correct, just as there is always a chance of convicting an innocent person in a court of law. The probability of a type I error is the **significance level** of the test. Data which fall into the 5% critical region are said to be **significant at the 5% level.**

If the critical region is in just one tail of the distribution, then the test is called a **one-tail test.** If the critical region is split equally between the two tails, then the test is called a **two-tail test.** Whether a test is a one-tail test or a two-tail test depends on the alternative hypothesis.

One-tail test

H_0 : mean $= \mu$
H_1 : mean $> \mu$

The critical region at the 5% level is

$X > \mu + 1.645\sigma$

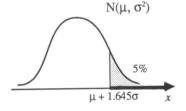

Two-tail test

H_0 : mean $= \mu$
H_1 : mean $\neq \mu$

The critical region at the 5% level is

$X < \mu - 1.96\sigma$ or $X > \mu + 1.96\sigma$

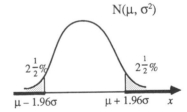

> Draw similar diagrams to show the critical regions of a Normal distribution for one and two-tail tests when the level of significance is
>
> (a)   1%   (b)   0.1%

In hypothesis testing, statisticians adopt the following convention to describe the significance of observed data.

- Data which occur in the critical region at the 5% level of significance are called *significant*.

- Data which occur in the critical region at the 1% level of significance are called *very significant*.

- Data which occur in the critical region at the 0.1% level of significance are called *highly significant*.

Example 1

Last year Lisbeth was elected president of the students' union when 40% of members supported her. She claims that her support has increased during her year in office. The college magazine selects 150 students at random for a survey and finds that 75 say that they will vote for her this year. Does this provide significant evidence for an increase in her support?

Solution

Assuming that her support is unchanged, if the number of students who support her in a random sample of 150 is r, then $R \sim B(150, 0.4)$.

$H_0 : p = 0.4$
$H_1 : p > 0.4$

Level of significance: 5%

The Normal approximation to the binomial is $X \sim N(60, 36)$.

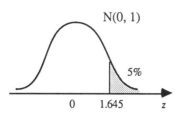

$$z = \frac{74.5 - 60}{\sqrt{36}} \approx 2.42$$

As the result of the survey falls in the critical region you should reject H_0 and conclude that there has been a significant increase in her support.

Has there been a 'highly significant' increase in her support?

5

The following result was established in *The Normal distribution*.

> **The Central Limit Theorem states that if** $X \sim N(\mu, \sigma^2)$
>
> **then the distribution of sample means is** $\bar{X} \sim N(\mu, \frac{\sigma^2}{n})$.

Example 2

You can buy a cup of 'cola' from a drinks machine. The amount dispensed, 300 ml, varies slightly. If X is the amount dispensed in millilitres, then $X \sim N(300, 10^2)$.

The operator samples four cups and accurately measures their contents. If the sample mean is significantly different from the expected value, she resets the machine.

Calculate the 'acceptable' range of values for the sample mean.

Solution

$H_0 : \mu = 300$
$H_1 : \mu \neq 300$

Level of significance: 5%

The distribution of sample means is Normally distributed: $\bar{X} \sim N(300, \frac{10^2}{4})$.

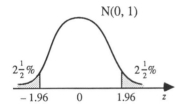
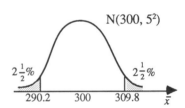

The region of acceptance is $300 - 1.96 \times 5 < \bar{X} < 300 + 1.96 \times 5$

is $290.2 < \bar{X} < 309.8$

Exercise 1

1. In a multiple choice question paper of 120 questions, each with five possible answers, what number of correct answers would lead you to accept that a candidate is **not** answering purely by guesswork? To answer this question, set up appropriate null and alternative hypotheses and test at a 5% significance level.

2. 3.14159265358979 ... shows the first fourteen decimal places of π. Is there any evidence to suggest that the number of even digits after the decimal point will be significantly different from the number of odd digits when the expansion is continued?

3. The breaking strain of a type of rope is Normally distributed with mean 1300 newtons and standard deviation 40 newtons. A sample of nine lengths gives the following results when tested.

1334 1264 1284 1308 1198 1244 1236 1204 1304 (newtons)

Is there significant evidence that the breaking strain is lower than expected, and if so, at what level of significance?

4. A machine produces ball-bearings whose diameters are Normally distributed with a mean 3.00 mm and standard deviation 0.05 mm. A random sample of 50 ball-bearings is found to have a mean of 3.01 mm. Does the machine need adjusting?

5. A farmer grows cabbages under stable greenhouse conditions. Their weights are Normally distributed with mean 0.85 kg and variance 0.04 kg². One year he tries out a new fertilizer and weighs a random sample of 60 cabbages to see if there has been a significant improvement in yield. He finds that the 60 cabbages have a mean weight of 0.91 kg. Would you describe this evidence as 'significant', 'very significant' or 'highly significant'?

6. A drug manufacturer claims that only 5% of patients experience any side-effects when given a new drug. In clinical trials, 250 patients were given the drug and 21 of them reported side-effects. Would you describe these results as significant at the 1% level?

7. In a manufacturing process, a machine produces rods which must have a diameter, x, between 7.9 mm and 8.1 mm.

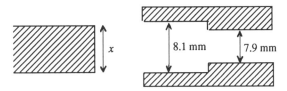

The rods are tested using the gauge shown in the diagram. Rods outside the required limits are 'wasted'. At the end of a day's production the manufacturer finds that 7% of the rods are 'wasted', 6.6% being too large and 0.4% being too small.

(a) If you can assume $X \sim N(\mu, \sigma^2)$, estimate μ and σ from the information given.

(b) If the machine is adjusted so that the mean is 8.0 mm, calculate the proportion of 'wasted' rods. (Assume the variance is unchanged.)

(c) A random sample of 10 rods is taken after the machine has been adjusted. The sample mean is 8.02 mm. Does the machine need readjusting?

1.5 Population proportions

Suppose that a proportion, p, of the members of a parent population possess a particular characteristic. As shown in *The Normal distribution*, if p_S is the proportion of the members of a large random sample of size n which possess the characteristic, then p_S has sampling distribution approximately

$$N\left(p, \frac{p(1-p)}{n}\right)$$

The ideas of significance testing can therefore be applied to population proportions and have particular relevance in the area of opinion polls. The modern importance of opinion polls largely stems from Dr. Gallup's successful prediction of the American election in 1936. Although there have been several notable failures since then, such as the incorrect forecasts for the United Kingdom general election of 1992, opinion polls , at least in theory, depend upon mathematical ideas of significance and properties of the Normal distribution. For example, one of the well-known claims for general election opinion polls is that they have a 'margin of error of 3%'. This is based upon the result proved in the next example.

Example 3

The support for a particular political party is approximately 40%. What size of sample is needed so that you can be 95% certain of predicting the actual support to within 3%?

Solution

For the Normal distribution, 95% of samples are within 1.96 s.d. of the mean.

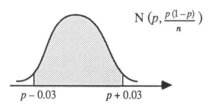

$$N\left(p, \frac{p(1-p)}{n}\right)$$

$p - 0.03 \qquad p + 0.03$

For the required certainty, 1.96 s.d. must correspond to 3% i.e.

$$1.96\sqrt{\left(\frac{p(1-p)}{n}\right)} = 0.03$$

$$\Rightarrow 1.96\sqrt{\left(\frac{0.4 \times 0.6}{n}\right)} \approx 0.03$$

$$\Rightarrow \frac{0.922}{n} \approx 0.0009$$

$$\Rightarrow \qquad n \approx 1024$$

In practice, you will find that many general election polls have a sample size of approximately 1000 and so 95% of such polls will be accurate to within 3%.

> **Support for the Liberal party is approximately 20%. What size of sample is needed to predict support for this party to within 3% with 95% certainty?**

Exercise 2

1. In one constituency, 46% of the votes cast were for Labour. Six months later an opinion poll was carried out in the area; 400 people were interviewed and 52% indicated that they would vote Labour. Has there been a significant increase in the Labour vote?

2. A survey of 400 randomly selected adults is held in a particular constituency a month before a general election and 144 indicate that they will vote Conservative. In the election the Conservative candidate polls 33.8% of the votes. Is there a discrepancy between the results of the poll and the election?

3. The manufacturers of Kleenrite claim that 50% of people prefer their product. In a public opinion survey of 200 people, 86 stated a preference for Kleenrite. Does this survey provide significant evidence that the manufacturers are overstating the preference for their product?

After working through this chapter you should:

1. understand the terms null hypothesis and alternative hypothesis;

2. be familiar with the symbols H_0 and H_1;

3. understand the meaning of a type I error and a type II error;

4. understand what is meant by level of significance;

5. know how to carry out a test of significance;

6. know when to use a one-tail test and when to use a two-tail test;

7. be able to apply a significance test to a population proportion.

The binomial distribution

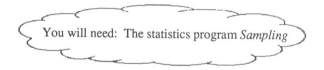

You will need: The statistics program *Sampling*

The *Sampling* program simulates the binomial distribution, B(n, p). If, for example, you would like to simulate what happens when you throw a loaded die sixty times, put *sample size* = 60 and *percentage* = 25% (this is the probability of 'showing a six' for a loaded die). You also have to state how many times you want the computer to carry out the simulation. For example, you might put *number of samples* = 200.

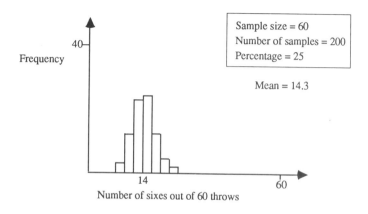

1. Carry out the simulation shown above and use it to estimate the probability of

   (a) precisely 14 sixes (b) fewer than 14 sixes.

2. Repeat question 1 two or three times and explain why your answers to 1(a) and 1(b) would be expected to vary slightly each time the simulation is carried out.

3. Carry out a similar simulation to show the number of sixes you get out of sixty throws when the die is 'fair'. Again, repeat the simulation two or three times. Use the results to estimate the probability of obtaining 14 or more sixes.

The following results were established in the unit *The Normal distribution*.

$$\text{For } R \sim B(n, p)$$

$$P(R = r) = \binom{n}{r} p^r (1-p)^{n-r} \text{ where } \binom{n}{r} = \frac{n!}{r!\,(n-r)!}$$

$$\text{mean} = np \text{ and variance} = np(1-p)$$

(continued)

4.   If $R \sim B(60, 0.25)$ calculate $P(R = 14)$. Comment on how your answer compares with your answer to question 1(a).

5.   If $R \sim B(60, 0.25)$ calculate the mean and variance of R.

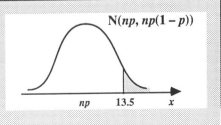

The Normal approximation to the binomial is often used to estimate probabilities such as $P(R \geq 14)$.

6.   If $X \sim N(np, np(1-p))$ is the Normal approximation to $R \sim B(n, p)$ explain why $P(R \geq 14) \approx P(X > 13.5)$.

7.   Use the Normal approximation to the binomial to estimate

   (a) $P(R \geq 14)$ where $R \sim B(60, \frac{1}{6})$

   (b) $P(R < 14)$ where $R \sim B(60, \frac{1}{4})$

8.   You can write a short program to calculate binomial probabilities on a computer or graphic calculator. (A short program is given at the back of this book.) Repeat question 7 using a program instead of the Normal approximation.

9.   Comment on any discrepancies between your answers to

   (a)   questions 1 and 3 and question 8 ;

   (b)   question 7 and question 8.

1. The following table was published in the *Times Educational Supplement* just before the 1992 general election.

PERCENTAGE OF TEACHERS WHO WOULD VOTE FOR EACH PARTY:			
1979	**Con**	**Lab**	**Lib**
Primary	59	27	14
Secondary	45	40	15
1983			
Primary	49	25	23
Secondary	39	27	31
1987			
Primary	24	22	52
Secondary	24	34	41
1992			
Primary	17	47	22
Secondary	17	48	22

© Times Newspapers Ltd. 1992

Suppose that, in 1992, the Liberal Democrats in a particular area of the country believed that support for them among local teachers was particularly strong.

If a random sample of 80 teachers in the area revealed that 25 intended to vote for the Liberal Democrats, could this have been used as significant evidence for their claim?

2. (a) The daily production of components at a factory had a mean of 1000 and a standard deviation of 20. In a 100 day period following the implementation of recommendations from a firm of management consultants, the factory produced 100 600 components. Has there been a significant improvement?

   (b) The daily production of a similar factory also has mean 1000 and standard deviation 20. It is decided to implement the same recommendations and to pay the consultants an additional fee if the production over a 100 day period exceeds 100 330.

   (i) What would be a 'type I error' for this example? Find the probability of a type I error.

   (ii) What would be a 'type II error' for this example? Find the probability of a type II error given that the mean daily production has been changed to 1004.

2 Student t-distribution

2.1 Large samples

In *The Normal distribution*, you met the result that if $X \sim N(\mu, \sigma^2)$ then, for a sample of size n, $\overline{X} \sim N(\mu, \frac{\sigma^2}{n})$.

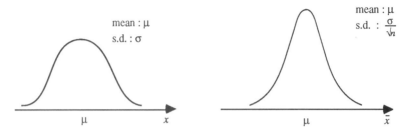

mean : μ
s.d. : σ

mean : μ
s.d. : $\frac{\sigma}{\sqrt{n}}$

The standardised variable representing the difference between the sample mean and the population mean is:

$$z = \frac{\overline{x} - \mu}{\frac{\sigma}{\sqrt{n}}}, \quad \text{where } Z \sim N(0, 1)$$

From the Central Limit Theorem, this standardised variable can be used even when the parent population is not Normally distributed providing the sample size is large.

> If a large sample of size n is taken from a population with mean μ and standard deviation σ, then the distribution of $z = \frac{\overline{x} - \mu}{\frac{\sigma}{\sqrt{n}}}$ is approximately N(0, 1).

In Chapter 1 you saw how to set up and test hypotheses against evidence gathered from statistical sampling. This type of testing is often used in research, quality control or to test the outcome of some change in production methods. Suppose, for example, that a market gardener changes to an organic method of growing cucumbers and is concerned that the cucumbers should be about the same size as those he grew in previous years.

Before using organic methods, a gardener kept detailed records and found that his cucumbers had a mean length of 35.0 cm. To check the lengths of his organically grown cucumbers, he takes a random sample of 100 and measures their lengths. He finds that the sample mean is $\overline{x} = 34.1$ cm and that $s_{n-1}^2 = 16.0$ cm².

Does this constitute evidence of a decrease in length? State carefully any assumptions you make.

Sometimes it is necessary to use data from a sample to estimate a population variance. In the case of the market gardener's cucumbers, the variance of the parent population was unknown and had to be estimated before the problem could be analysed. The following result, demonstrated in *The Normal distribution*, enables a population variance to be estimated from a sample variance.

$$s_{n-1}^2 = \frac{n}{n-1} s_n^2 \quad \text{is an } \textit{unbiased} \text{ estimator of } \sigma^2.$$

The error in using the sample variance to estimate σ^2 is small when the sample size is large and the following result can be applied .

$$\text{For large samples, if } z = \frac{\bar{x} - \mu}{s_{n-1}/\sqrt{n}} \text{ then } Z \sim N(0, 1).$$

Example 1

A biologist is investigating whether the use of chemical sprays by farmers adversely affect wild life. It is known that twenty years ago the mean weight of wood mice was 55.0 g. No information on the variance is available. The biologist catches 50 wood mice and finds that their mean weight $\bar{x} = 53.9$ g and that $s_{n-1}^2 = 25.3$ g^2. Is this significant evidence of a decrease in weight?

Solution

$H_0 : \mu = 55.0$
$H_1 : \mu < 55.0$

Level of significance: 5%

Reject H_0 if $z < -1.645$ where $z = \dfrac{\bar{x} - \mu}{\left(\dfrac{s_{n-1}}{\sqrt{n}}\right)}$

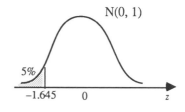

Here $z = \dfrac{53.9 - 55}{\sqrt{\left(\dfrac{25.3}{50}\right)}} = -1.546$

As $-1.546 > -1.645$, H_0 is **not** rejected. The evidence is not significant.

2.2   Small samples

In Section 2.1, dealing with large samples, you saw how the distribution of $\frac{\bar{x}-\mu}{s_{n-1}/\sqrt{n}}$ is approximately N(0, 1) even if the parent population is not Normally distributed. However, decisions often have to be made on evidence gathered from small samples. In particular, there are many instances where it is necessary to use a small sample to estimate a population variance.

The statistician William S. Gossett, also known by his pen-name 'Student', was particularly concerned with finding ways of dealing with decision-making when the only available information came from small samples. He was able to develop results for small samples, but only for parent populations which are Normally distributed. For X Normally distributed, with mean μ, Gossett investigated the distribution of $\frac{\bar{x}-\mu}{s_{n-1}/\sqrt{n}}$ for small n. He called this new distribution the t-distribution. The next tasksheet gives you the opportunity to replicate his work.

TASKSHEET 1 – *Student t-distribution*

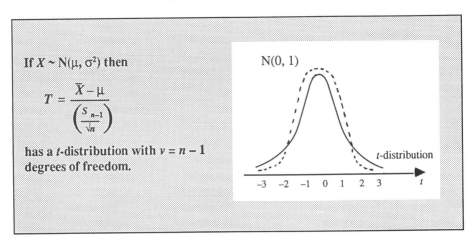

If $X \sim N(\mu, \sigma^2)$ then

$$T = \frac{X - \mu}{\left(\frac{S_{n-1}}{\sqrt{n}}\right)}$$

has a t-distribution with $v = n - 1$ degrees of freedom.

The random variable:

$$T = \frac{\bar{X} - \mu}{\left(\frac{S_{n-1}}{\sqrt{n}}\right)}$$

is the ratio of two random variables, $\bar{X}$ and S_{n-1}. These two random variables are not completely independent as the statistic $\bar{x}$ has to be calculated **before** you calculate s_{n-1}. It is because of this one constraint on the n elements in the sample that the variable S_{n-1} (and hence T) is said to have $n - 1$ degrees of freedom.

Although it is possible to use numerical methods to make accurate probability statements about any t-distribution, the process is tedious and tables of values for the family of t-distributions have therefore been compiled. (These tables are found in the back of most statistics texts and you will find them at the back of this book together with tables of the standard Normal distribution.)

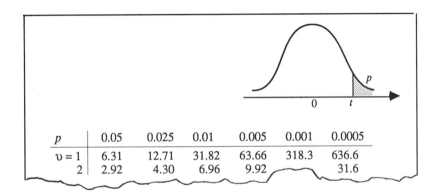

p	0.05	0.025	0.01	0.005	0.001	0.0005
$\upsilon = 1$	6.31	12.71	31.82	63.66	318.3	636.6
2	2.92	4.30	6.96	9.92		31.6

The table gives values of υ in the left hand column. The values of t corresponding to various probabilities, p, appear in the body of the table. Note that the table is designed for use in one-tail tests.

When $\upsilon = 8$ and $p = 0.025$, you can see from the table that $t = 2.31$.

(a) Draw a diagram to show this information.

(b) Explain carefully what this information tells you about the distribution of sample means.

(c) Look at the last line in the t-distribution table. Explain how (and why) these values relate to the corresponding points on the standard Normal distribution.

For practical purposes, the difference between a t-distribution and a standard Normal distribution is negligible for values of υ greater than 30.

For sample size $n < 30$, use:

$$t = \frac{\bar{x} - \mu}{\left(\frac{s_{n-1}}{\sqrt{n}}\right)}$$

where T has a t-distribution with degrees of freedom $\upsilon = n - 1$

For sample size $n \geq 30$, use:

$$z = \frac{\bar{x} - \mu}{\left(\frac{s_{n-1}}{\sqrt{n}}\right)}$$

where $Z \sim N(0, 1)$

For small samples it is necessary to assume that X is Normally distributed.

Example 2

It is claimed that a small packet of raisins contains 14.1 grams on average. The quality controller at the packing plant rejects a batch if she believes that the average weight of packets in the batch is less than 14.1 grams. She selects a random sample of 5 packets from a particular batch and weighs the contents.

x (grams) : 12.9   14.7   13.2   13.9   14.0

Is the evidence significant? Should she reject the batch?

Solution

$H_0 : \mu = 14.1$

$H_1 : \mu < 14.1$

Level of significance: 5%

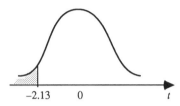

Assume that the weight, X, is Normally distributed. The variance of the population has to be estimated from a small sample and so $\dfrac{\bar{x} - \mu}{(s_{n-1}/\sqrt{n})}$ has a t-distribution with 4 degrees of freedom. Reject H_0 if $t \leq -2.13$.

The sample gives $\bar{x} = 13.74$ and $s_{n-1} = 0.709$ (to 3 d.p.)

So $t = \dfrac{13.74 - 14.1}{(0.709/\sqrt{5})} = -1.135$ (to 3 d.p.)

As $-1.135 > -2.13$ the quality controller should accept H_0 and **not** reject the batch.

Exercise 1

1. From the table, find the value of t which would be critical in

    (a) a one-tail test, sample size 6, at the 1% level;

    (b) a two-tail test, sample size 15, at the 5% level.

2. To test the effect of an irradiation process on apples, 10 pairs were chosen and one in each pair was irradiated. The pairs were then left in the same conditions and the time before rot set in was noted. The time differences in days for each pair ('treated' – 'untreated') were:

    x (days) : 30   7   51   120   16   34   –8   –74   –17   56

    Does the test show a significant difference in the times at the 10% level?

3. It is claimed by the manufacturer that a hearing aid battery lasts for 1000 hours with the hearing aid used at full volume. A random sample of 200 batteries is tested and found to have a mean life of 997 hours with $s_{n-1} = 13$ hours. The tester asserts that the manufacturer's claim is false. Is this fair?

   TASKSHEET 2E – *Plotting t-distributions*

18

2.3 Confidence intervals

You met the idea of a confidence interval for the mean in *The Normal distribution*. The *t*-distribution is often used instead of a Normal distribution when calculating a confidence interval if the only available information about a population is provided by the sample itself.

Students on a biology field trip to the Norfolk Broads are asked to investigate the local population of common frogs. During the afternoon they catch just 12 frogs. They weigh them and obtain the following data.

Weight (grams) : 85 125   95 160 95 70 110 105 115   50 140 145

The students calculate the mean weight as $\bar{x} = 107.9$ grams, but are not sure how good an estimate this is for the frog population of the area.

They assume that weight has a Normal distribution so that the statistic

$$t = \frac{\bar{x} - \mu}{\left(\frac{s_{n-1}}{\sqrt{12}}\right)}$$

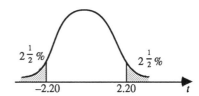

has a *t*-distribution with $\upsilon = 11$ degrees of freedom.

From a *t*-distribution table, $P(-2.20 < T < 2.20) = 0.95$.

Another way of looking at this is to say that 95% of samples of size 12 would give a value of the random variable T such that

$$-2.20 < t < 2.20.$$

A 95% confidence interval for the mean weight can therefore be obtained from:

$$-2.2 < \frac{\bar{x} - \mu}{\left(\frac{s_{n-1}}{\sqrt{12}}\right)} < 2.2$$

(a) Show how this inequality can be rearranged to give:

$$\bar{x} - 2.2\left(\frac{s_{n-1}}{\sqrt{12}}\right) < \mu < \bar{x} + 2.2\left(\frac{s_{n-1}}{\sqrt{12}}\right)$$

(b) Calculate s_{n-1} for the sample of frogs.

(c) Hence show that the 95% confidence interval for the mean weight of the population of frogs is : $87.7 < \mu < 128.1$.

(d) Calculate the 90% confidence interval.

Suppose that a parent population has a Normal distribution and that a random sample of size n has been obtained. If σ has to be estimated from the data in the sample, then a t-distribution with $n-1$ degrees of freedom must be used when determining a confidence interval for the population mean μ.

$$\bar{x} - t\left(\frac{s_{n-1}}{\sqrt{n}}\right) < \mu < \bar{x} + t\left(\frac{s_{n-1}}{\sqrt{n}}\right)$$

For example, for a 95% confidence interval, t is the value in the t-distribution which has an area $p = 0.025$ to the right of it.

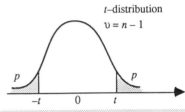

Exercise 2

1. At a packing station, ten peaches are picked out at random from a large batch of the same variety and are found to have the following weights in grams:

    160 105 125 145 110 140 125 150 115 145

    (a) Find a 90% confidence interval for the mean.

    (b) Find 95% and 99% confidence intervals.

2. Thirty university students volunteer to take part in an investigation into the effect of alcohol has on a person's ability to carry out simple tasks. The students are split at random into two groups of fifteen and both groups are asked to perform a test of manual dexterity. However, the members of one group consumed a quantity of alcohol half an hour before being tested. The times taken to complete the test are given in the table.

    Without alcohol x(s) 12.2, 8.3, 14.7, 10.7, 9.8, 12.5, 13.2, 13.0, 9.6, 11.3 11.9, 10.8, 16.2, 11.0, 10.1

    With alcohol y(s) 12.3, 14.8, 17.2, 19.7, 10.2, 16.7, 21.5, 9.9, 11.7, 19.7, 19.5, 20.0, 24.3, 13.5, 25.9

    Calculate 95% confidence intervals for each sample and comment on your findings.

2.4   Matched pairs *t*-test

The technique of matched pairs testing is particularly important. You have already met the idea in Question 2 of Exercise 1. A further example is described below.

A manufacturer claims that a new slimming aid enables you to lose weight without the need to diet. A consumer association doubts the validity of this claim and selects eight volunteers to test it. Each volunteer was weighed before and after a course of treatment.

	A	B	C	D	E	F	G	H
weight before (kg)	76.3	80.1	77.3	69.5	83.4	72.4	64.0	79.3
weight after (kg)	75.1	79.5	78.5	68.1	83.3	72.1	62.7	79.0

To see if this provides significant evidence in support of the manufacturer's claim, you can analyse the **change in weight**. However, it is necessary to assume that this variable, the change in weight, is Normally distributed.

	A	B	C	D	E	F	G	H
weight change (kg) x :	−1.2	−0.6	+1.2	−1.4	−0.1	−0.3	−1.3	−0.3

Assume that X is Normally distributed, $X \sim N(\mu, \sigma^2)$

$H_0 : \mu = 0$ the treatment makes no difference
$H_1 : \mu < 0$ there has been a decrease in weight

Level of significance : 5%

(a)   Calculate $\bar{x}$ and s_{n-1} for the sample of weight changes, and use a *t*-test to show that the sample does not provide significant evidence in support of the manufacturer's claim.

(b)   Does this prove that the manufacturer's claim is false?

Exercise 3

1. Lengths of pipe were buried in soil so that the corrosive effect of the soil on the pipe could be measured. Half the length of each pipe was given a special coating to protect it against corrosion. The following data show the measured corrosion on the coated and uncoated parts in different types of soil.

Soil type	A	B	C	D	E	F	G	H	I
Uncoated	63	42	69	64	79	77	52	85	63
Coated	47	30	73	65	81	71	32	82	51

Carry out a t-test to see if the sample provides very significant evidence (at the 1% level) to support the claim that coating pipes offers some protection against corrosion.

2. A group of trainee managers were given a memory task. The group was then given a course of instruction on how to improve recall. They were then tested again using a similar task.

Their results were:

Trainee manager	A	B	C	D	E	F	G	H	I	J	K	L	M	N	O
Score before	11	12	9	7	17	14	13	15	12	16	14	12	13	14	14
Score after	12	11	10	10	16	16	16	19	13	15	18	15	14	14	17

Is the apparent improvement in score significant? (State any assumptions you make.)

3. Two weight reducing diets, A and B, are to be compared. Ten matched pairs of overweight people are selected and diet A randomly assigned to one of each pair, the other being assigned diet B. At the end of a six week period the weight losses are as shown:

Pair	1	2	3	4	5	6	7	8	9	10
Weight loss on diet A (kg)	7	4	3	10	6	8	12	14	9	10
Weight loss on diet B (kg)	10	5	3	13	7	6	16	13	10	6

Is there a significant difference in the weight losses?

After working through this chapter you should:

1. know that the statistic $t = \dfrac{\bar{x} - \mu}{\left(\frac{s_{n-1}}{\sqrt{n}} \right)}$ has a *t*-distribution

   with $\upsilon = n - 1$ degrees of freedom when $X \sim N(\mu, \sigma^2)$;

2. appreciate the original work of W.S. Gossett ('Student') in investigating the distribution of the random variable *T*;

3. know how a *t*-distribution differs from a standard Normal distribution for small samples;

4. appreciate why a *t*-distribution can be approximated by a standard Normal distribution for a sample of size 30 or more;

5. know how to use a *t*-distribution to test a null hypothesis;

6. know how to use a *t*-distribution to calculate a confidence interval for a population mean;

7. know how to test for a significant difference using a sample of matched pairs.

Student t-distribution

Gossett worked for the Guinness brewery in the early 1900s. It was the policy of the company that employees should not publish under their own name so Gossett adopted the pen-name 'Student' and is now best known by this name. 'Student' was particularly interested in the distribution of the statistic:

$$t = \frac{\text{sample mean} - \text{population mean}}{\text{estimated standard error}} = \frac{\bar{x} - \mu}{\left(\frac{s_{n-1}}{\sqrt{n}}\right)}$$

He investigated the distribution of t by calculating $\bar{x}$ and s_{n-1} (and hence t) for a large number of samples of size $n = 4$. The samples were all picked at random from a Normally distributed population with known mean and variance.

He chose as his parent population one which had been investigated some years previously by the statistician W.R. Macdonell and published in *Biometrika* in 1901. Macdonell had shown that the height distribution of 3000 criminals, obtained from the records of Scotland Yard, was in very close agreement with what would be expected from a Normal distribution.

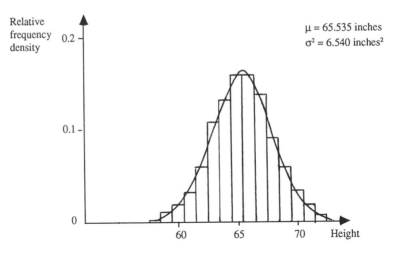

'Student' wrote down the 3000 heights in random order and, taking each consecutive set of 4 as a sample, he calculated 750 values of t.

1.   Suppose the values in one of 'Student's' samples were 62, 63.5, 65 and 62.5 inches. Calculate the values of $\bar{x}$, s_{n-1}^2 and t for this sample.

2.   (a)   Calculate the value of $z = \dfrac{\bar{x} - \mu}{\sqrt{\left(\frac{\sigma^2}{n}\right)}}$ for the sample in question 1.

      (b)   Explain why you would expect $Z \sim N(0, 1)$.

3.   In what way would you expect the variance of the distribution of T to differ from that of Z?

(continued)

The results 'Student' obtained were published in *Biometrika* in 1908 and are shown in the histogram. The theoretical *t*-distribution for samples of size 4 is superimposed.

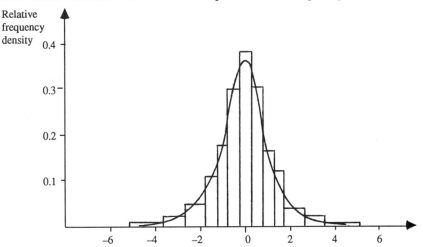

4. What feature of the histogram shows that the distribution is **not** a standard Normal distribution?

It can be shown that the equation of a *t*-distribution is given by:

$$f(t) = c_\upsilon \left(1 + \frac{t^2}{\upsilon}\right)^{-\left(\frac{\upsilon+1}{2}\right)} \quad \text{where the parameter } \upsilon = n - 1$$

and where c_υ is a constant such that $\displaystyle\int_{-\infty}^{\infty} f(t)\,dt = 1$.

5. (a) Shown that when $n = 4$ (i.e. $\upsilon = 3$) the equation of the *t*-distribution is given by:

$$f(t) = c_3 \left(1 + \frac{t^2}{3}\right)^{-2}$$

   (b) Use a numerical method of integration to evaluate $\displaystyle\int_{-\infty}^{\infty} \left(1 + \frac{t^2}{3}\right)^{-2} dt$.

   (c) Hence explain why the constant $c_3 = 0.368$ (to 3 s.f.).

'Student' was unable to prove that a *t*-distribution has this equation. It was some time later that his friend and colleague, Sir Ronald A. Fisher, supplied a proof and it is for this reason that the *t*-distribution is sometimes referred to as the 'Student-Fisher distribution'. However, it is usually called simply the 'Student *t*-distribution'. The method 'Student' used to investigate areas under the *t*-distribution was very time consuming because he did not have access to the sort of computing power taken for granted today.

6E. Use the random number generator on a computer or graphic calculator to select 750 samples of size 4 from a N(0, 1) distribution. Program the computer (or graphic calculator) to calculate the value of *t* for each sample and hence draw a histogram similar to the one obtained by 'Student'. (You will find a suitable program at the back of the book.)

Plotting t-distributions

The equation of a t-distribution is:

$$f(t) = c_\upsilon \left(1 + \frac{t^2}{\upsilon}\right)^{-\frac{(\upsilon+1)}{2}}$$

where c_υ is a constant such that $\displaystyle\int_{-\infty}^{\infty} f(t)\,dt = 1$

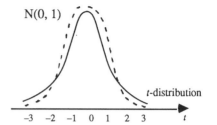

1. (a) Use a numerical method to show that $\displaystyle\int_{-\infty}^{\infty} \left(1 + \frac{1}{5}t^2\right)^{-3} dt \approx 2.634$.

   (b) Explain why this shows that $c_5 = 0.380$ (to 3 s.f.)

   (c) Use a similar method to evaluate c_υ when $\upsilon = 10$, 20 and 50.

2. (a) Write down the equation of the t-distribution when the degrees of freedom are:

   (i) $\upsilon = 3$ (ii) $\upsilon = 5$ (iii) $\upsilon = 10$

   (iv) $\upsilon = 20$ (v) $\upsilon = 50$

   (b) Use a graph plotter to plot the graph of the standard Normal variable,

   $$f(z) = \frac{1}{\sqrt{(2\pi)}}\, e^{-\frac{1}{2}z^2}$$

   (c) Superimpose the graphs of the t-distributions obtained in (a).

   (d) Describe and discuss the significance of what you find.

As a point of mathematical interest, it can be shown that the t-distribution with $\upsilon = 1$ has equation:

$$f(t) = \frac{1}{\pi(1 + t^2)}$$

This distribution is known as the Cauchy distribution and is of particular interest because it can further be shown that while its mean is zero (by symmetry) its variance is infinitely large.

1. A sample has $\bar{x} = 6.71$ and $s_{n-1} = 0.68$. The null hypothesis is $\mu = 6.5$, where μ is the mean of the parent population. The alternative hypothesis is $\mu \neq 6.5$.

   What significance can be ascribed to the result if the sample size is

   (a) 10   (b) 25   (c) 50   (d) 100?

2. The table below gives the weight of a sample of potatoes.

Weight in g (interval centre)	60	100	140	180	220	260	300	340	380	420
Frequency	10	20	15	5	3	1	1	2	1	2

   Calculate estimates of the mean and s_{n-1} for the sample.

   Assuming that this is a random sample from a large consignment of potatoes, find 95% confidence limits for the mean weight of potatoes in the consignment.

3. A machine is cutting off shelving components with a nominal length of 30.0 cm. In a random sample of eight, the lengths in cm are found to be

   $$30.04, \ 30.02, \ 30.08, \ 29.96, \ 30.06, \ 29.98, \ 30.10, \ 30.08$$

   Find 95% confidence limits for the mean length. Is the result consistent with the given nominal length?

4. The quality controller of a unit producing silicon chips has noted that in the past 87% of the output has been satisfactory. She takes a batch of 15 at random and finds that 4 of them fail her tests. Does this indicate a deterioration in the unit's output?

3 Two sample tests

3.1 Comparing two means

In Chapter 2 you saw how to test hypotheses about a population mean using a sample drawn from the population. In this chapter you will be concerned with making comparisons between two population means using two samples, one taken from each of the populations.

For some time, environmentalists have been urging a change from leaded to lead-free petrol. Although motorists are usually keen to be 'green' they might hesitate to change to unleaded if it is expensive to do so. Even if unleaded is a little cheaper they might suspect that leaded will give more miles per gallon.

A company conducts an experiment to investigate how a new lead-free petrol, which does not require an engine conversion, compares with regular four-star. Most of the company's employees have a company car of a particular make and model. A sample of ten of them is selected at random and asked to use four-star petrol for the duration of the trial. Another random sample of ten is asked to use the new unleaded.

> **Suppose ten representatives, who travel large distances, were asked to use the new petrol while ten office staff who just drive to and from work each weekday were asked to use four-star. Why would this not be a valid trial?**

For the period of the trial the twenty employees all calculate their rate of petrol consumption in miles per gallon. The resulting data are as follows:

leaded: X 35.4 34.5 31.6 32.4 34.8 31.7 35.4 35.3 36.6 36.0

unleaded: Y 29.7 29.6 32.1 35.4 34.0 34.8 34.6 34.8 32.7 32.2

From data previously available to the company they decide to assume

- rates in miles per gallon are Normally distributed;
- the s.d. is 1.8 miles per gallon, for all types of petrol.

So it may be assumed that

$$X \sim N(\mu_X, 1.8^2), \quad Y \sim N(\mu_Y, 1.8^2)$$

(a) **What are the probability distributions for the populations of sample means $\bar{X}$ and $\bar{Y}$?**

(b) **Calculate $\bar{x}$ and $\bar{y}$ for the sample data. Check that $\bar{x} > \bar{y}$. If not, it is not worth continuing the test!**

A suitable null hypothesis is that the average rate is the same for both types of petrol.

$$H_0 : \mu_X = \mu_Y$$

A suitable alternative is that the average rate is higher with leaded than with unleaded.

$$H_1 : \mu_X > \mu_Y$$

If the null hypothesis is true and the distributions of X and Y have equal means then you would expect the difference $\bar{x} - \bar{y}$ to be close to zero. What has to be found is how far from zero the difference must be before the null hypothesis is rejected. To carry out a hypothesis test you need to know the distribution of $\bar{X} - \bar{Y}$.

You will need the program *Ncomb*.

The variables used in the program are X and Y where

$$X \sim N(\mu_X, \sigma_X^2) \text{ and } Y \sim N(\mu_Y, \sigma_Y^2)$$

The computer generates 300 values of a selected combination of X and Y and plots the results on a histogram together with the sample mean and variance.

(a) **Input values of μ_X, μ_Y, σ_X^2, σ_Y^2 of your own choice and investigate the distribution of $X - Y$.**

(b) **Repeat (a) several times, using different means and variances for X and Y.**

(c) **In your opinion, is the distribution of $X - Y$ Normal? Explain your answer.**

(d) **How are the mean and variance of $X - Y$ related to the means and variances of X and Y?**

The results for the difference of two Normally distributed variables can be summarised as follows.

If $W \sim N(\mu_w, \sigma_w^2)$ and $V \sim N(\mu_v, \sigma_v^2)$ are independent, then

$$W - V \sim N(\mu_w - \mu_v, \sigma_w^2 + \sigma_v^2).$$

That is

- **the difference $W - V$ between two Normally distributed variables W and V is also Normally distributed;**

- **the mean value of $W - V$ is the *difference* of the means of W and V;**

- **the variance of $W - V$ is the *sum* of the variances of W and V.**

Example 1

W has a Normal distribution with mean 20 and s.d. 3, V has a Normal distribution with mean 15 and s.d. 2. What is the distribution of $W - V$?

Solution

$W - V$ has Normal distribution, with

mean $20 - 15 = 5$, variance $3^2 + 2^2 = 13$.

$W - V \sim N(5, 13)$.

The hypothesis test to be developed in the next section is based upon the following three assumptions. In the case of large samples, the second and third of these assumptions can be waived. For large samples, sample means are distributed approximately normally and the variance of the parent population can be estimated with reasonable accuracy.

- A sample is drawn from the first population under consideration and **completely independently** a sample is drawn from the second population.

- Both populations have Normal distributions.

- The variances of both populations are known.

All three assumptions hold in the case of the petrol trial.

3.2   Testing the equality of two means

You are now in a position to solve the problem of the petrol trial, using the standard procedure.

$H_0 : \mu_X = \mu_Y$

$H_1 : \mu_X > \mu_Y$

Distribution of $\bar{X} - \bar{Y}$ if H_0 is true.

Distribution of $\bar{X} - \bar{Y}$ if H_1 is true.

$\bar{X} - \bar{Y}$ has a Normal distribution: $\bar{X} - \bar{Y} \sim N(\mu_X - \mu_Y, \frac{1.8^2}{10} + \frac{1.8^2}{10})$

If $z = \dfrac{(\bar{x} - \bar{y}) - (\mu_X - \mu_Y)}{\sqrt{(\frac{1.8^2}{10} + \frac{1.8^2}{10})}}$, then $Z \sim N(0, 1)$

The company is investigating whether the new petrol gives a lower rate in miles per gallon, so a 5% one-tail test should be applied. H_0 will be rejected at the 5% level if $z > 1.645$.

Assuming H_0, $\mu_X - \mu_Y = 0$, $\bar{x} - \bar{y} = 1.38$ and $\sqrt{(\frac{1.8^2}{10} + \frac{1.8^2}{10})} = 0.805$.

So $z = \dfrac{1.38}{0.805} = 1.71$.

Since $1.71 > 1.645$, H_0 is rejected at the 5% level. There is evidence that the unleaded petrol gives a lower rate in miles per gallon than the four-star leaded, though the evidence is not strong.

Find P(Z > 1.71).

In general, the sizes of the two samples compared need not be equal. The various tests based upon two samples may be summarised as follows.

> **Suppose that X is Normally distributed with mean μ_X and variance σ_X^2 and Y is Normally distributed with mean μ_Y and variance σ_Y^2. Then the null hypothesis $H_0 : \mu_X = \mu_Y$ may be tested against any *one* of these three posssible alternatives H_1.**
>
> **$\mu_X \neq \mu_Y$ or $\mu_X > \mu_Y$ or $\mu_X < \mu_Y$**

In the test, assume independent samples of size m for X and of size n for Y. Then the test statistic is

$$z = \frac{\bar{x} - \bar{y}}{\sqrt{\left(\frac{\sigma_X^2}{m} + \frac{\sigma_Y^2}{n}\right)}}$$

where $\bar{x}$ is the mean of the sample from X and $\bar{y}$ is the mean of the sample from Y. This value of z is compared with the value in the table of areas under the standard Normal curve.

The diagrams show when H_0 is rejected (and H_1 accepted) at the 5% level.

$H_1 : \mu_X \neq \mu_Y$ $\qquad\qquad$ $H_1 : \mu_X > \mu_Y$ $\qquad\qquad$ $H_1 : \mu_X < \mu_Y$

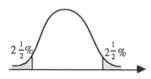 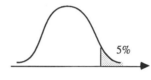 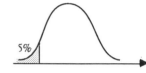

Sometimes you may have to estimate the variance of the parent population from that of the sample.

Example 2

The weights of the first 100 children born in a large city in a given year are recorded and analysed, with these results.

No. of girls 56, with mean weight 3.258 kg, variance of sample 0.1473 kg²
No. of boys 44, with mean weight 3.489 kg, variance of sample 0.2675 kg²

Does this constitute evidence that in the city the birth weight of boys is greater than that of girls?

Solution

It may be assumed that the 56 girls and 44 boys are independent random samples from Normally distributed populations.

The standard procedure is followed. Samples with means $\bar{b}, \bar{g}$ and variances s_B^2 and s_G^2 are taken from the background populations B and G of boys and girls respectively.

$H_0 : \mu_B = \mu_G$

$H_1 : \mu_B > \mu_G$

Level of significance: 5%

$$\bar{B} - \bar{G} \sim N\left(\mu_B - \mu_G, \frac{\sigma_B^2}{44} + \frac{\sigma_G^2}{56}\right)$$

Since the variances of B and G are not given they can be estimated as $\frac{44}{43} s_B^2$ and $\frac{56}{55} s_G^2$ respectively, using the formula $\frac{ns^2}{n-1}$ for an unbiased estimator for σ^2.

As the sample sizes are large, you can assume that $Z \sim N(0, 1)$ where

$$z = \frac{\bar{b} - \bar{g}}{\sqrt{\left(\frac{s_B^2}{43} + \frac{s_G^2}{55}\right)}}$$

H_0 is to be rejected if $z > 1.645$.

$b = 3.489$, $g = 3.258$, $s_B^2 = 0.2675$ and $s_G^2 = 0.1473$

So, $z = \frac{0.231}{0.0943} = 2.45$

Since $2.45 > 1.645$, H_0 is rejected.

The given data constitute evidence that the birth weight of boys in the city is greater than that of girls.

For sufficiently large samples the distribution of sample means is Normal even when the parent population is not Normally distributed.

Example 3

Glitto and Pufco manufacture Christmas light bulbs. Each company claims that its bulbs have the longest life. In an experiment to investigate whether there is a significant difference in the average lives of the two makes of bulb, 100 bulbs are randomly selected from each production line and tested.

Glitto's bulbs have a mean life of 798 hours and it is known from data previously obtained that the variance is 7800 hours². Pufco's bulbs have a mean life of 826 hours with variance 9000 hours². However, Pufco's mean was obtained using a sample of only 98 bulbs because two were broken after the sample had been taken. Settle the dispute between Glitto and Pufco.

Solution

Sample means of **large** samples from a parent population with **any** distribution are Normally distributed, by the Central Limit Theorem. In other respects, the requirements for using the standard test apply. Let X and Y be the lives in hours of bulbs made by Glitto and Pufco respectively.

$H_0 : \mu_X = \mu_Y$

$H_1 : \mu_X \neq \mu_Y$

Level of significance: 5%

$$\bar{X} - \bar{Y} \sim N\left(\mu_X - \mu_Y , \frac{\sigma_X^2}{100} + \frac{\sigma_Y^2}{98}\right)$$

$Z \sim N(0, 1)$ where $z = \dfrac{\bar{X} - \bar{Y}}{\sqrt{\left(\frac{\sigma_X^2}{100} + \frac{\sigma_Y^2}{98}\right)}}$

H_0 is rejected if $z < -1.96$ or $z > 1.96$.

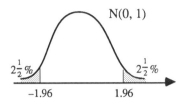

Substituting $\bar{x} = 798$, $\bar{y} = 826$, $\sigma_X^2 = 7800$, $\sigma_Y^2 = 9000$

$$z = \frac{-28}{13.0} = -2.15$$

Since $-2.15 < -1.96$, H_0 is rejected in favour of H_1. There is a significant difference in the average lifetimes of the two makes of bulb.

> **Find $P(Z < -2.15)$**

Exercise 1

In each of the following examples start by stating suitable null and alternative hypotheses in words before you express them algebraically.

1. The ages at which men married for the first time were recorded for samples of 80 men in country A and 100 men in country B. The mean for A was found to be 24.5 years and that for B was 26.1 years. Previous larger studies found the standard deviations for A and B to be 3.2 and 2.8 years respectively. Is there evidence that men in B marry for the first time later in life than those in A? (Use a 1% significance level.)

2. A company has two models of car in its fleet. A sample of 20 of the first model was found to have an average annual maintenance cost of £540 while a sample of 11 of the second model had an average of £710. National figures show that the standard deviation of annual maintenance costs for the first and second models are £90 and £110 respectively. The company is thinking of changing all its fleet to cars of the first model to save on maintenance costs. Would you advise them to do so? (Use a 5% significance level.) What assumptions did you have to make to carry out this hypothesis test?

3. An educational psychologist suspects a logical thinking test of being biased against girls. She administers the test to a random sample of 50 boys and 50 girls. The average scores are 68.9 for the boys and 61.8 for the girls. It is known that the variance of test scores for boys is 144 whereas the variance for girls is 196. Test whether the psychologist's suspicions are true. (Use a 1% significance level.)

4. A market gardener grows a particular variety of cucumber in two plots. He uses chemical fertilisers and pesticides on the first plot but the cucumbers in the second plot are grown organically.

In a particular year a sample of 50 cucumbers from the first plot has mean length 36.5 cm and a sample of 50 from the organic plot has mean length 35 cm. Assuming the variance of cucumbers of both types to be 16 cm² test whether using organic methods significantly changes the average length of the cucumbers. (Use a 5% significance level.)

5. The energy expended in 24 hours by 12 underweight and 10 overweight women is shown below.

	MJ/day										
Underweight	6.1	7.1	10.9	10.1	7.5	8.4	7.6	7.7	8.2	7.9	6.5	7.5
Overweight	12.8	11.9	9.9	10.0	9.7	9.7	9.2	11.7	12.8	8.9		

Previous data show the standard deviation to be 1.20 MJ/day for underweight women and 1.41 MJ/day for overweight women. It is also known that energy consumption has a Normal distribution. Use the data shown above to test whether overweight women expend more energy than underweight women on average. (Use a 5% significance level.)

3.3　Confidence intervals

In Example 3 it was found that the mean lifetimes of two types of light bulbs were different. A confidence interval for the actual difference can be found using a result from *The Normal distribution*.

You know that if $X \sim N(\mu, \sigma^2)$ then $P(\mu - 1.96\sigma < X < \mu + 1.96\sigma) = 0.95$

This inequality can be rearranged to give $P(X - 1.96\sigma < \mu < X + 1.96\sigma) = 0.95$

You can therefore be 95% confident that an interval $(x - 1.96\sigma, x + 1.96\sigma)$ does in fact contain the mean, μ. This is the **95% confidence interval** for the mean.

A similar results holds for the difference between two means.

> If $\bar{X} \sim N\left(\mu_X, \dfrac{\sigma_X^2}{n}\right)$ and $\bar{Y} \sim N\left(\mu_Y, \dfrac{\sigma_Y^2}{m}\right)$ then $\bar{X} - \bar{Y} \sim N\left(\mu_X - \mu_Y, \dfrac{\sigma_X^2}{n} + \dfrac{\sigma_Y^2}{m}\right)$
>
> The 95% confidence interval for $\mu_X - \mu_Y$ is
>
> $$\left(\bar{x} - \bar{y} - 1.96\sqrt{\left(\dfrac{\sigma_X^2}{n} + \dfrac{\sigma_Y^2}{m}\right)},\ \bar{x} - \bar{y} + 1.96\sqrt{\left(\dfrac{\sigma_X^2}{n} + \dfrac{\sigma_Y^2}{m}\right)}\right)$$

> **(a)**　Use the above result to find a 95% confidence interval for $\mu_X - \mu_Y$ in Example 3.
>
> **(b)**　Find a 99% confidence interval for $\mu_X - \mu_Y$.

Exercise 2

1.　A sample of size 50 from a Normal distribution with known variance 25 has mean 10.3. A sample of size 72 from a second Normal distribution with known variance 36 has mean 8.2. Construct a 95% confidence interval for the difference between the mean of the first Normal distribution and that of the second.

2.　Construct a 95% confidence interval for the difference in daily energy expenditure between underweight and overweight women. Use the data given in question 5 of Exercise 1.

3.　Use the data given in sections 3.1 and 3.2 to construct a 90% confidence interval for the difference between the mean miles per gallon using leaded petrol and the mean miles per gallon using unleaded petrol.

4.　A random sample of 100 low-tar cigarettes of brand A is found to have a mean tar content of 9.9 mg. A random sample of 100 low-tar cigarettes of brand B has a mean tar content of 8.9 mg. Assuming the standard deviation to be 1.6 mg for both brands, find a 99% confidence interval for the difference between the mean tar content of brand A and that of brand B.

3.4 Pooled variance estimator

In the pharmaceutical industry, comparisons must often be made between medicines. Suppose a particular pharmaceutical company manufactures two treatments, A and B, for diverticulosis, a disorder of the alimentary canal. With the co-operation of local hospitals, a statistician from the company randomly selects a sample of 15 patients who are receiving treatment A and another sample of 15 patients receiving B.

The experiment consists of administering a marker pellet to each patient and measuring the time taken for the pellet to pass through the alimentary canal. 3 of the patients receiving treatment B either do not keep their appointments on the days on which the experiment is conducted or do not record the time, reducing the second sample size to 12. The data which result from the experiment are as follows.

Treatment	Time in hours
A	44 51 52 55 60 62 66 68 69 71 71 76 82 91 108
B	52 64 68 74 79 83 84 88 95 97 101 116

It would be reasonable to assume that the times for the two treatments are Normally distributed. However, the two sample test developed in this chapter cannot be applied to these results because of the small sample sizes and the fact that the population variances are unknown.

By analogy with the methods used in Chapter 2, you might think of applying the t-test with the samples being used to estimate the population variances. The only examples considered in this unit will be ones where the two samples can be assumed to come from populations with a **common** variance. In such cases, the variance is estimated using a particular combination of the sample variances. The general method will be illustrated using the example of the two treatments for diverticulosis.

(a)   **Find the mean and variance, s_A^2 , of the times for A**

(b)   **Find the mean and variance, s_B^2 , of the times for B.**

Suppose that the two populations from which the times for A and B have been sampled both have variance σ^2. Possible unbiased estimators for σ^2 are $\frac{15}{14} s_A^2$ and $\frac{12}{11} s_B^2$

Either of these estimators could be used but it is more reliable to use a combination of both s_A^2 and s_B^2. The **pooled variance estimator** is based upon the weighted average of s_A^2 and s_B^2 , the weightings depending upon the number of elements in each set.

$15 s_A^2 + 12 s_B^2$ has mean $14 \sigma^2 + 11 \sigma^2$ and so a suitable unbiased estimator is

$$\frac{15 s_A^2 + 12 s_B^2}{25}$$

Explain the above derivation of the pooled variance estimator.

In general, the pooled variance estimator is calculated as follows.

> Suppose $X \sim N(\mu_X , \sigma^2)$ and $Y \sim N(\mu_Y , \sigma^2)$. Suppose further that a sample of X of size n_X has variance s_X^2 and a sample of Y of size n_Y has variance s_Y^2 . The pooled variance estimator for σ^2 is the unbiased estimator
> $$\frac{n_X s_X^2 + n_Y s_Y^2}{n_X + n_Y - 2}$$

(a)   **For the samples of times for treatments A and B given earlier, find three separate unbiased estimators for the population variance using**

          (i)   **sample A only;**

          (ii)   **sample B only;**

          (iii) **a pooled estimator.**

(b)   **Explain why the three estimates are different. In what sense is the pooled estimate likely to be the 'best' of the three estimates?**

3.5 Two sample *t*-test

Suppose that in advance of the experiment considered in Section 3.4, the statistician thinks that treatment A is more effective than B, which would be shown by the marker pellets taking less time to pass through the alimentary canal. The significance test is then:

$H_0 : \mu_A = \mu_B$

$H_1 : \mu_A < \mu_B$

Level of significance: 5%

The samples are such that $\bar{a} = 68.4 \quad s_A^2 = 253.31$

$$\bar{b} = 83.42 \quad s_B^2 = 285.08$$

If $A \sim N(\mu_A, \sigma^2)$, then $\bar{A} \sim N(\mu_A, \frac{\sigma^2}{15})$. Similarly, $\bar{B} \sim N(\mu_B, \frac{\sigma^2}{12})$ and so $\bar{A} - \bar{B} \sim N(\mu_A - \mu_B, (\frac{1}{15} + \frac{1}{12})\sigma^2)$.

The test statistic $\dfrac{\bar{a} - \bar{b}}{\sigma \sqrt{(\frac{1}{15} + \frac{1}{12})}}$ has a standard Normal distribution. However, since σ is unknown it must be replaced by the sample estimate, s. Then, as in Chapter 2,

$$\frac{\bar{a} - \bar{b}}{s \sqrt{(\frac{1}{15} + \frac{1}{12})}}$$

has a *t*-distribution. It can be proved that the number of degrees of freedom is $(15 - 1) + (12 - 1) = 25$.

> **Complete the significance test for the two treatments. Carefully state your conclusion.**

> Suppose two small samples of sizes n_1 and n_2 have mean values $\bar{x}_1$ and $\bar{x}_2$. If it is reasonable to assume that the two populations are Normal and have the same variance, then an appropriate statistic to test for the equality of the means of the two populations is
>
> $$t = \frac{\bar{x}_1 - \bar{x}_2}{s \sqrt{(\frac{1}{n_1} + \frac{1}{n_2})}}$$
>
> where s^2 is the pooled sample variance and t has a *t*-distribution with $n_1 + n_2 - 2$ degrees of freedom.

Example 4

A biologist wishes to find out if the habitat of a particular small animal affects its weight. Traps are set by the side of a lake and near the top of a hill. The biologist suspects that those animals by the lakeside will weigh more. The weights of the animals, in grams, are as follows:

lakeside	25.7	27.3	28.5	29.6	30.2	30.4	31.6
hill top	24.2	24.6	27.3	28.2	28.9		

Does the habitat affect the weights of the animals?

Solution

Assume the lakeside weights have a distribution $X \sim N(\mu_X, \sigma^2)$.

Assume the hill top weights have a distribution $Y \sim N(\mu_Y, \sigma^2)$.

$H_0 : \mu_X = \mu_Y$

$H_1 : \mu_X > \mu_Y$

The biologist carries out a one-tail test at the 5% level.

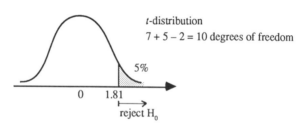

t-distribution
$7 + 5 - 2 = 10$ degrees of freedom
5%
0   1.81
reject H_0

$\bar{x} = 29.04, \quad s_X^2 = 3.51, \quad n_X = 7$

$\bar{y} = 26.64, \quad s_Y^2 = 3.62, \quad n_Y = 5$

The pooled variance estimate of σ^2 is

$$\frac{7 \times 3.51 + 5 \times 3.62}{7 + 5 - 2} \approx 4.267$$

Then $t = \dfrac{29.04 - 26.64}{\sqrt{4.267} \ \sqrt{(\frac{1}{7} + \frac{1}{5})}}$

≈ 1.98

As $1.98 > 1.81$, H_0 is rejected in favour of H_1. There is significant evidence that the lakeside animals are heavier.

Exercise 3

1. In an experiment to determine the relative effectiveness of two diet plans, 6 people were assigned to plan A and 8 to plan B. The weight losses (in kilograms) were as shown:

   Plan A $\bar{x}_A = 3.3$ $s_A^2 = 1.2$ $n_A = 6$

   Plan B $\bar{x}_B = 4.1$ $s_B^2 = 1.7$ $n_B = 8$

   (a) Assuming that the population variances are equal, find the pooled estimate for this common variance.

   (b) Conduct a two-tail t-test to see if there is a significant difference in the mean weight losses for the two diets.

2. During a particular fishing holiday, trout caught in two rivers, the Arn and the Bate, had the following lengths in centimetres.

Arn	27.5	26.1	26.4	27.1		
Bate	25.6	24.3	24.9	25.7	26.0	26.8

   (a) Assuming that both populations of trout have the same variance, find a pooled estimate of this variance.

   (b) Is there significant evidence that trout from the Arn have a greater average length than those from the Bate?

3. A metallurgist wishes to determine if there is a significant difference in the amount of an impurity in silver purified by two different processes. For ten samples, she obtained the following results:

	Percentage of impurity					
Process 1	3.4	2.7	2.5	3.8		
Process 2	3.7	3.5	4.0	3.4	3.4	3.0

   What should she conclude?

4. The times taken (in minutes) for two children to complete an arcade game are as shown:

Alex	2.10	2.22	2.15	2.10	2.17		
Jackie	2.11	2.03	2.08	2.04	2.08	2.14	2.11

   How significant is the evidence that the two players differ in ability at the game?

After working through this chapter you should:

1.   be able to apply a significance test of the hypothesis that the means of two populations are equal, against any one of the three possible alternative hypotheses;

2.   know that a test using a Normally distributed statistic can be made if

   •   the samples are independent,
   •   the parent populations are Normally distributed,
   •   the variances of the parent populations are known,

   and understand why the latter two conditions may be waived in the case of large samples;

3.   know that a test using a t-distribution can be made if

   •   the samples are independent,
   •   the parent populations are Normally distributed,
   •   the parent populations have the same variance;

4.   be able to find confidence intervals for the difference between two means.

1. Two examiners, A and B, mark the same set of 50 papers. The mean mark given by A is 42.8 and that given by B is 43.9. From data obtained on the distribution of scores for the examination it may be assumed that the variance for both examiners is 10.8.

    (a) What evidence is there that A is a harder marker than B?

    (b) Calculate the 98% confidence interval for the difference between the average mark awarded by A and that awarded by B.

2. In a well-known investigation, conducted in 1902, the ornithologist Latter compared the lengths of eggs laid by cuckoos in the nests of wrens and hedge sparrows. He obtained these values, in millimetres.

Eggs from nest of wren	Eggs from nest of hedge sparrow
19.8	22.0
22.1	23.9
21.5	20.9
20.9	23.8
22.0	25.0
21.0	24.0
22.3	23.8
21.0	21.7
20.3	22.8
20.9	23.1
22.0	23.5
22.0	23.0
20.8	23.0
21.2	23.1
21.0	

Assuming that the lengths of eggs laid in both kinds of nests are Normally distributed, use the two sample test of this chapter to investigate Latter's claim that cuckoos are able to adapt their eggs to the host bird.

Comment on the validity of the test for these data.

4 Non-parametric tests

4.1 The sign test

Hypotheses have so far been tested either against a binomial distribution or against a Normal distribution. However, it is not always reasonable to assume that a distribution is Normal. For example, in a traffic survey where the lengths of time between cars passing a certain point on a main road were recorded, it was found that the times varied from 0.1 to 15.8 seconds with 'most' being between 2 and 6 seconds.

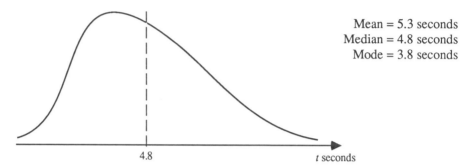

Mean = 5.3 seconds
Median = 4.8 seconds
Mode = 3.8 seconds

The researcher wants to carry out a quick check to see if the average time between cars is the same on a different day of the week. She chooses the median as her measure of average, measures a random sample of 36 time gaps between cars and marks a '+' if a gap is greater than 4.8 seconds and a ' − ' if it is less. Her results are:

$$+ - + - + - + + - + - - + + - + + - - + + \ - + - + + + - + + - + + - + +$$

Her hypotheses are

H_0 : The median = 4.8

H_1 : The median ≠ 4.8   a two-tail test

Level of significance : 5%

(a) **If r is the number of plus signs, why is it reasonable for her to assume that $R \sim B(36, \frac{1}{2})$?**

(b) **Does her sample provide significant evidence in support of the alternative hypothesis?**

(c) **In theory, why is there zero probability that a gap is precisely equal to the median value?**

(d) **In practice, why are you likely to find that some data items are equal to the median?**

The type of test used by the researcher is called the **sign test**. The major advantage of the sign test is that no assumptions need to be made regarding the 'shape' of the population distribution. The test is said to be **non-parametric.**

- The sign test can be used when the null hypothesis is that a population *median* has a particular value.

- Measurements are recorded as being *above* the median (+) or as being *below* the median (–).

- The plus and minus signs are assumed to occur with equal probability so that the number of pluses, R, has distribution $B(n, \frac{1}{2})$.

- For a Normal distribution (or any symmetrical distribution) the mean and median are equal. The sign test can therefore be used to test a null hypothesis about the mean of a Normal distribution without the need for any assumption about the variance.

If a sample value is **equal** to the assumed median, then that value is ignored and the sample size is reduced.

Example 1

The time that secretaries stay at one branch of a firm have been found to have a median value of 42 months. From another branch, a sample of times (in months) are

$$36 \quad 15 \quad 42 \quad 60 \quad 10 \quad 20 \quad 39 \quad 40 \quad 14$$

Is this significant evidence that the median time at the second firm is less than 42 months?

Solution

H_0 : median = 42
H_1 : median < 42

Level of significance: 5%

The signs are

$$- \quad - \quad 0 \quad + \quad - \quad - \quad - \quad - \quad -$$

Then, discarding the zero, $R \sim B(8, \frac{1}{2})$ with $r = 1$.

$$P(R \le 1) = \left(\frac{1}{2}\right)^8 + 8\left(\frac{1}{2}\right)^8 \approx 0.035$$

H_0 is rejected at the 5% level. There is significant evidence that the staying time at the second branch is lower.

Exercise 1

1.

> Britain's 8 million-plus children aged five to sixteen, get an average £1.82 a week, an 8 per cent increase on last year with inflation now at 4.5 per cent. Scottish children get £2.07 a week, while those in London and the South average about £1.79.

Guardian, March 3 1992, Source: Gallup

A sample of 20 children from a village in Suffolk showed that their weekly pocket money was:

   60p, £1.20, £3, £2.40, £1, £1, £4.20, £3.50, £2, 70p, £1.50,
   £2.30, £3.50, £5, £6.50, £1.60, £2.80, £2, £2.50, 50p

Does the sample reveal a significant difference from what was found by the Gallup poll? State your null and alternative hypotheses together with any assumptions you may make.

2. The average (median) life of the African locust is 28 days in the wild. A school breeds 14 locusts as part of a biology course and notes how long each survives in captivity. The results are:

   12, 17, 22, 22, 23, 23, 23, 24, 25, 25, 28, 30, 37, 38 (days)

What conclusions (if any) can be drawn from these results?

3. A maker claims that a particular computer game improves hand-eye co-ordination. To test this a student selected ten fellow students at random, all of whom said they did not usually play the game.

She asked them to perform a standard hand-eye co-ordination task and gave each a score according to how well they performed. They then spent every lunch hour for a week playing the computer game. The following week they were tested again for co-ordination to see if they had improved.

The results were:

Student	:	A	B	C	D	E	F	G	H	I	J
First score	:	56	87	32	80	76	56	49	69	61	51
Second score	:	58	87	52	85	71	60	72	71	70	57
Improvement	:	+2	0	+20	+5	−5	+4	+23	+2	+9	+6

Write down null and alternative hypotheses and use the sign test to decide if there is significant evidence to support the maker's claim.

4.2 The Wilcoxon signed-rank test

For each of the hypothesis tests considered in the first three chapters, it is necessary either to assume that the population distribution is known or that the sample size is sufficiently large that the Central Limit Theorem can be applied.

> **What has to be assumed about the population distribution for a two sample *t*-test?**

The sign test, considered in Section 4.1, is an example of a **non-parametric test.** It can be applied irrespective of the 'shape' of the population distribution.

> **A non-parametric test is one which does *not* assume any knowledge of the distribution involved. Many such tests concentrate on the median of an unknown distribution.**

The sign test ignores the magnitudes of the differences from the median. In 1945, Frank Wilcoxon refined the test for roughly symmetrical distributions by taking these magnitudes into account. This test is known as the **Wilcoxon signed-rank test** or the **T test**. As an example of this procedure, consider the data on the locusts bred in captivity.

Lifetime (days): 12 17   22   22   23   23   23   24   25   25   28   30   37   38

Consider, at the 5% level, the hypotheses

H_0 : median = 28
H_1 : median ≠ 28

The signed differences from the median, in ascending order of magnitude, are as shown. The sample value equal to the median has been ignored.

$$2 \quad -3 \quad -3 \quad -4 \quad -5 \quad -5 \quad -5 \quad -6 \quad -6 \quad 9 \quad 10 \quad -11 \quad -16$$

These 13 differences are then assigned ranks from 1 to 13. When two or more sample values have equal magnitude they are given the average of the relevant ranks. In the case of the locusts the ranks are as shown.

Difference	2	−3	−3	−4	−5	−5	−5	−6	−6	9	10	−11	−16
Rank	1	2.5	2.5	4	6	6	6	8.5	8.5	10	11	12	13

The sum of the ranks corresponding to positive differences is then $1 + 10 + 11 = 22$.

> **Find the sum of the ranks corresponding to negative differences.**

The smaller of the two sums is called T. In the case, $T = 22$.

Wilcoxon showed how to calculate the probabilities of each value of T. Critical values of T for various sample sizes and significance levels are given in a table at the back of this book.

> (a) Explain how you would expect the size of T to provide evidence for or against the null hypothesis.
>
> (b) Complete the hypothesis test for the locusts.

The Wilcoxon signed-rank test can be used to test for a median of a roughly symmetrical distribution.

- Calculate the signed differences from the median.

- Discard any zero value and, ignoring sign, rank the remaining differences in order of magnitude. Assign the average rank to any values which are equal in magnitude.

- Calculate T, the smaller of the sums of 'positive' ranks or 'negative' ranks.

- Compare your value of T with that given in a table of critical values of T for various sample sizes.

Exercise 2

1. The ages (in years) of first offenders for violent crime is believed to have a median of 24. A prison officer finds that the ages for 12 recently committed offenders are

   23   27   28   20   26   26   24   17   38   24   33   39

   Do these data provide significant evidence that the median is greater than 24?

2. For students at a sixth form college, the median mark on a standardised aptitude test is expected to be approximately 60. A teacher has a group of seven new students whose marks are

   48   70   18   20   53   47   76

   Do these scores provide significant evidence that the new entry has a lower median score than 60?

3. For ten days an executive timed her journey to and from work. On eight days, travelling to work took longer by 8, 3, 2, 4, 6, 5 , 6 and 7 minutes. On the remaining two days the journey to work was shorter by 1 and 4 minutes. Is there significant evidence for a difference in journey times to and from work?

After working through this chapter you should:

1. know that is meant by a non-parametric test;

2. appreciate why it is sometimes necessary to apply a non-parametric test;

3. be able to test a population median by using either the sign test or the Wilcoxon signed-rank test.

1.   The standardised scores for pupils at a school have a median mark of 100. It is claimed that pupils with names at the start of the alphabet are likely to do better because they receive more attention from teachers. The first eight pupils in the alphabet have the following scores

   114, 107, 92, 99, 101, 123, 142, 101

   (a)   Carry out a sign test to test the hypothesis that the median score is 100.

   (b)   Suppose the distribution of scores can be approximated by a Normal distribution with mean 100 and standard deviation 15. Test the hypothesis that the mean score is 100.

   (c)   Comment on your answers to (a) and (b).

2.   The manufacturers of a new paint claim that it dries in two hours. A painter believes that it tends to take longer and records the drying times on his next twelve jobs. In minutes, these are as follows:

   130   140   160   100   150   180   170   80   140   190   160   90

   (a)   What would be suitable null and alternative hypotheses to which a non-parametric test could be applied?

   (b)   To decide if there is significant evidence to reject the manufacturer's claim, carry out

   (i)   a sign test;

   (ii)   a Wilcoxon signed-rank test.

   (c)   Comment on your answers to (b).

5 Correlation and regression

5.1 Bivariate distributions

In earlier chapters you have concentrated on populations of a single variable, such as height or mass. Sometimes it is interesting to study the relationships between a pair of variables, in which case a **bivariate distribution** is involved. For example, each adult in the country has a height X cm and a mass of Y kg; the ordered pair (X, Y) is said to have a bivariate distribution.

Example 1

Display graphically the following data, of mass and foot area, recorded for a sample of 20 South American snails of the species Biomphalaria glabrata.

Mass (gm), X	0.64	0.21	0.85	0.53	0.18	0.06	0.20	0.07	0.01	0.05
Foot (mm²), Y	29	16	35	25	20	7	13	7	3	10

Mass (gm), X	0.02	0.01	0.21	0.81	0.53	0.18	0.06	0.20	0.07	0.01
Foot (mm²), Y	4	1	16	35	25	20	7	13	7	1

Solution

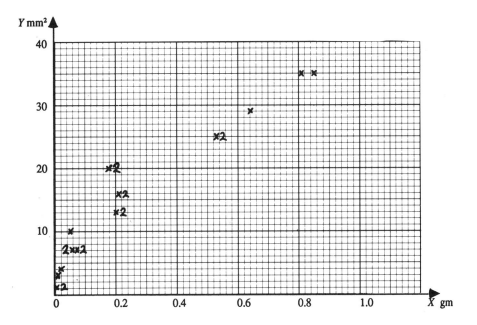

The graph of a bivariate distribution such as the one in Example 1 is called a **scatter plot**.

> What do the 2's on the plot signify?

The points in the scatter plot clearly lie close to a straight line; there is an approximate linear relationship between the variables. In such a case the variables are said to be **positively correlated.**

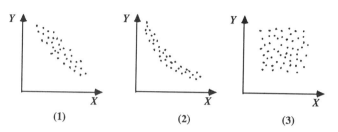

Other possibilites are illustrated by these scatter plots.

(1) (2) (3)

How would you describe the relationship between X and Y in these three cases?

The object of this chapter is to determine when it is reasonable to use a linear approximation for the relationship between two variables and, when it is, to find the equation of the **'line of best fit'.** Using the methods developed you will be able to describe precisely the relation between the variables in a given sample from a bivariate distribution. When the relation may be taken as linear you will be able to make predictions based on the linear relationship.

TASKSHEET 1 – *Covariance*

Suppose that a sample $\{(x_1, y_1), (x_2, y_2), \ldots (x_n, y_n)\}$ taken from the bivariate distribution (X, Y) has sample mean $(\bar{x}, \bar{y})$. Then

$$\text{Cov}(X, Y) = \frac{1}{n} \sum_{1}^{n} (x_i - \bar{x})(y_i - \bar{y})$$

is called the *sample covariance* between X and Y.

5.2   The product moment correlation coefficient

A sample covariance close to zero indicates that there is no correlation between the variables. A 'large' positive covariance indicates a positive correlation and a 'large' negative covariance a negative correlation. (How large depends on the sizes of the variables and their variances.)

Example 2

Heights X in a bivariate distribution (X, Y) are at present recorded in metres. What would be the effect on a sample covariance if they were recorded in centimetres?

Solution

Any height in metres, X_i, would be replaced in the calculation by a height in centimetres, $100X_i$. The covariance would change from

$$\frac{1}{n} \sum (x_i - \bar{x})(y_i - \bar{y}) \text{ to } \frac{1}{n} \sum (100x_i - 100\bar{x})(y_i - \bar{y})$$

The latter expression may be written as $\frac{100}{n} \sum (x_i - \bar{x})(y_i - \bar{y})$, showing that the sample covariance has increased by a factor of 100.

> **What happens to Cov (X, Y) if all the values of X are multiplied by 5 and all the values of Y by 4?**

As you might expect, a subjective assessment of 'largeness' is not acceptable. Sample covariances must be standardised to give an objective statistical measure.

> The standard measure of correlation is called Pearson's product moment correlation coefficient and is denoted by r.
>
> It is found by dividing the sample covariance by the product of the sample standard deviations of X and Y, i.e.
>
> $$r = \frac{\text{Cov } (X, Y)}{s_X s_Y}$$

> **What happens to r if all the values of X are multiplied by 5 and all the values of Y by 4?**

In calculating r it is useful to note that

$$\text{Cov}(x, y) = \frac{1}{n} \sum (x_i - \bar{x})(y_i - \bar{y})$$

$$= \frac{1}{n} \left(\sum x_i y_i - \bar{y} \sum x_i - \bar{x} \sum y_i + n\bar{x}\,\bar{y} \right)$$

$$= \frac{1}{n} \left(\sum x_i y_i - n\bar{x}\,\bar{y} - n\bar{x}\,\bar{y} + n\bar{x}\,\bar{y} \right)$$

$$= \frac{1}{n} \left(\sum x_i y_i - n\bar{x}\,\bar{y} \right)$$

> Explain why (a) $\sum \bar{x}\,\bar{y} = n\bar{x}\,\bar{y}$, (b) $\bar{y} \sum x_i = n\bar{x}\,\bar{y}$

Hence

$$r = \frac{\text{Cov}(X, Y)}{s_X s_Y} = \frac{\frac{1}{n}\left(\sum x_i y_i - n\bar{x}\bar{y}\right)}{\sqrt{\left[\frac{1}{n}\left(\sum x_i^2 - n\bar{x}^2\right)\frac{1}{n}\left(\sum y_i^2 - n\bar{y}^2\right)\right]}}$$

$$= \frac{\sum x_i y_i - n\bar{x}\bar{y}}{\left(\sum x_i^2 - n\bar{x}^2\right)\left(\sum y_i^2 - n\bar{y}^2\right)}$$

Example 3

Find the Pearson correlation coefficient for the bivariate distribution in Example 1.

Mass (gm), X	0.64	0.21	0.85	0.53	0.18	0.06	0.20	0.07	0.01	0.05
Foot (mm²), Y	29	16	35	25	20	7	13	7	3	10

Mass (gm), X	0.02	0.01	0.21	0.81	0.53	0.18	0.06	0.20	0.07	0.01
Foot (mm²), Y	4	1	16	35	25	20	7	13	7	1

Solution

From the data, $\sum x_i y_i = 124.73$, $\sum x_i^2 = 2.6032$, $\sum y_i^2 = 6514$,

$\bar{x} = 0.245$, $\bar{y} = 14.7$, $n = 20$

Hence

$$r = \frac{124.73 - 20 \times 0.245 \times 14.7}{\sqrt{[(2.6032 - 20 \times 0.245^2)(6514 - 20 \times 14.7^2)]}}$$

$$= \frac{52.7}{\sqrt{(1.4027 \times 2192.2)}} = 0.95$$

54

It may be proved algebraically that r always lies between -1 and $+1$. One method of demonstrating this result is given in question 6E of Exercise 1. Statements about meanings of covariances including vague ideas of 'largeness' can now be replaced by more precise expressions in terms of the standardised statistic.

> If $r \approx 1$, there is strong positive correlation.
> If $r \approx -1$, there is strong negative correlation.
> If $r \approx 0$, X and Y are uncorrelated.

When $r \approx 1$ you will expect points (x, y) to lie close to a line with positive gradient; when $r \approx -1$ the same applies except that the gradient is negative. Thus, in Example 1, the fact that the points lie very close to a straight line is signified by the closeness of r (which is 0.95) to 1.

Exercise 1

1. The sea and air temperatures on a Florida beach were recorded at midday each Monday for 10 weeks. The data were as follows:

Sea $X°C$	19	22	18	19	21	22	18	18	17	16
Air $Y°C$	29	34	27	29	33	35	28	27	26	25

    (a) Plot these data on a scatter plot.

    (b) Calculate r and comment on the result.

2. Plot the following sets of data on a scatter plot, marking set 1 with crosses and set 2 with points.

Set 1 X	1	4	5	7	Set 2 X	0	2	5	6
Y	11	5	3	-1	Y	20	12	0	-4

    Calculate r for each set and comment on the values.

3. An investigation is carried out to see if there is a positive correlation between mathematical ability and verbal reasoning ability. The following data show (maths score, verbal reasoning score) for fourteen 12-year-olds.

    (15, 18) (19, 18) (23, 19) (19, 22) (18, 21) (26, 22) (22, 25)
    (22, 17) (23, 17) (32, 26) (28, 29) (29, 23) (28, 24) (27, 23)

    (a) Calculate r.

    (b) Do you think the two scores are positively correlated?

4. The period, T s, was recorded for seven pendulums of different lengths, l cm, with the following results:

l cm	10	20	30	40	50	60	70
T s	0.63	0.90	1.10	1.27	1.42	1.56	1.68

(a) Calculate r for the data.

(b) Draw a scatter plot.

(c) Do you think the relationship between l and T is linear?

5. Draw a scatter plot of the four points

$$(1, 1) \ (1, 3) \ (3, 1) \ (3, 3)$$

Calculate r and explain its value.

6E (a) Explain why, for real numbers a and b,

$$a^2 + b^2 \geq 2ab$$

(b) Hence show that if the numbers x_i and y_i are real,

(i) $(x_1^2 + x_2^2)(y_1^2 + y_2^2) \geq (x_1 y_1 + x_2 y_2)^2$

(ii) $(x_1^2 + x_2^2 + x_3^2)(y_1^2 + y_2^2 + y_3^2) \geq (x_1 y_1 + x_2 y_2 + x_3 y_3)^2$

(c) Generalise the results in part (b) and hence show that

$$[\text{Cov } (X, Y)]^2 \leq s_X^2 \, s_Y^2,$$

and so explain why $-1 \leq r \leq 1$.

5.3 Correlation and causation

Correlation coefficients are eagerly calculated by researchers in many fields ranging from social science to agriculture. Generally, they are attempting to prove that a change in one thing leads to a change in another – that increasing unemployment has caused an increase in crime or that the less space a pig has the more profit will be made.

In fact, a result $r \approx 1$ or $r \approx -1$ may be interpreted in any one of three ways. If say, Y increases as X increases,

- the increase in X may have caused the increase in Y, or vice versa,
- the two increases may have a common cause, or
- the increases may be causally unrelated.

Since the three categories given exhaust all the possibilities it is reasonable to conclude that, on its own, a result $r \approx 1$ or $r \approx -1$ gives no information about causation.

To be fair to scientific researchers they are well aware of this and would not attempt to base conclusions just on the value of a correlation coefficient.

> (a) **In which of the three categories would you place the connection between weight and height?**
>
> (b) **In the 1980's there was a steady increase in the student population of Sheffield. In the same town, there was also a steady increase in cases of thefts of cars. Into which of the categories above would you place this example?**

5.4   A line of best fit

Once you have established the likelihood of a linear relationship between two variables you may need to find the equation of the line involved.

TASKSHEET 2 – *Moderating exam marks*

The technique used to determine mathematically the equation of a line of best fit is called **regression**. Often, in collecting data from a bivariate distribution, the x data are thought of as being under the control of the experimenter and hence independently chosen. On the other hand, the y values will then depend on these x values. Because y is then the dependent variable you will usually want to estimate values of y for given values of x. Hence, the equation you usually require is found by 'regressing Y on X', taking the x values as in the data and working out the difference between theoretical and observed values of y.

Suppose that you have evidence of a linear relationship $y = a + bx$.

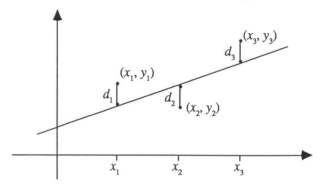

If the points (x_i, y_i) were exactly on the line you would expect

$$y_1 = a + bx_1, y_2 = a + bx_2, \ldots$$

The difference between a value of y in the data set and its expected value is the deviation

$$d_i = y_i - (a + bx_i), \; i = 1, 2, \ldots, n$$

The technique involves choosing a and b in such a way as to minimise $\sum_1^n d_i^2$.

> **Why would it not be sensible to try to minimise $\sum_1^n d_i$?**

The technique of minimising $\sum_i d_i^2$ is called **least squares regression**.

5.5 Equation of a line of best fit

The line of best fit for the regression of Y on X is mathematically defined as the line $y = a + bx$ for which $\sum_{1}^{n} (y_i - (a + bx_i))^2$ is minimum. From this definition, the following result can be derived.

> The equation of the line of best for the regression of Y on X is $y = \hat{a} + \hat{b}x$ where
>
> $$\hat{b} = \frac{\text{Cov}(X, Y)}{\text{Var}(X)} \quad \text{and} \quad \hat{a} = \bar{y} - \hat{b}\bar{x}$$
>
> This equation enables you to calculate the expected value of y for a given value of x.

Example 4

(a) For the distribution of Example 1, find the equation of the line of best fit for the regression of Y on X.

Mass (gm), X	0.64	0.21	0.85	0.53	0.18	0.06	0.20	0.07	0.01	0.05
Foot (mm²), Y	29	16	35	25	20	7	13	7	3	10

Mass (gm), X	0.02	0.01	0.21	0.81	0.53	0.18	0.06	0.20	0.07	0.01
Foot (mm²), Y	4	1	16	35	25	20	7	13	7	1

(b) Hence predict the foot area of a snail of mass 0.40 g.

Solution

(a) In Example 3 it was found that

$$\sum x_i y_i = 124.73, \quad \sum x_i^2 = 2.6032, \quad \bar{x} = 0.245, \quad \bar{y} = 14.7, \quad n = 20, \quad r = 0.95$$

Hence

$$\hat{b} = \frac{124.73 - 20 \times 0.245 \times 14.7}{2.6032 - 20 \times (0.245)^2} = \frac{53.7}{1.40} = 37.6$$

$$\hat{a} = 14.7 - 37.6 \times 0.245 = 5.50$$

The equation of the line of best fit is

$$y = 5.50 + 37.6x$$

59

(b)   When $x = 0.40$ the expected value of y is

$$5.50 + 37.6 \times 0.40 = 20.5$$

You would expect the foot area to be about 20 mm².

Some calculators enable you to find $\hat{a}$ and $\hat{b}$ with very little effort. You should find how to use your calculator for least squares regression lines and check the solution of Example 4.

   TASKSHEET 3 – *Estimating exam marks*

Exercise 2

1.   It is thought that reaction time correlates strongly with heart rate. Twelve surgeons take varying amounts of a drug affecting the heart rate to test this conjecture. The resulting data were as follows.

Heart rate x (beats/min)	134	133	132	123	118	110	98	90	84	80	80
Reaction time y (ms)	438	455	467	505	531	557	541	562	591	603	617

(a)   Is there a strong correlation between Y and X?

(b)   Show the data on a scatter plot.

(c)   Find the equation of the Y on X least squares regression line.

(d)   Draw the line on your scatter plot.

(e)   Predict the reaction time of a surgeon whose heart rate is 95 beats/min.

(f)   You are asked to predict the reaction time of a surgeon whose heart rate is 60 beats/min. Comment on this request.

2.   A tomato grower uses different amounts of fertilizer in each of twelve experimental beds, which are otherwise identical. The following data result.

Amount of fertilizer x (g)	10	12	14	16	18	20	22	24	26	28	30	32
Yield of tomatoes y (kg)	2	2	2	3	4	3	4	3	5	6	7	9

(a)   Calculate the product moment correlation coefficient r.

(b)   Find the equation of the regression line $y = \hat{a} + \hat{b}x$.

(c)   Is it appropriate to use the line to model the data?

5.6   Regressing X on Y

As noted earlier, it is usual for x to be the independent variable and y the dependent variable. Sometimes, though, there is no clearly independent variable and you may want to use regression to calculate expected values of x for given values of y. To find the equation of the line of best fit for regression of X on Y you must minimise the sum of squares of differences between each x value and its expected value if $x = c + dy$.

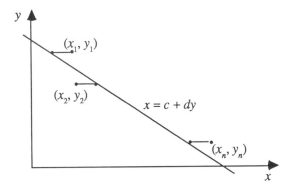

By symmetry with the result for regression of Y on X, the required equation is $x = \hat{c} + \hat{d}y$, where

$$\hat{d} = \frac{\text{Cov } (X, Y)}{\text{Var } (Y)} \text{ and } \hat{c} = \bar{x} - \hat{d}\bar{y}$$

Exercise 3

1.   Use the data of Example 1 to regress the mass of a snail (x g) on its foot area (y mm^2)

Mass (gm), X	0.64	0.21	0.85	0.53	0.18	0.06	0.20	0.07	0.01	0.05
Foot (mm^2), Y	29	16	35	25	20	7	13	7	3	10

Mass (gm), X	0.02	0.01	0.21	0.81	0.53	0.18	0.06	0.20	0.07	0.01
Foot (mm^2), Y	4	1	16	35	25	20	7	13	7	1

Draw a scatter plot of the data and show this regression line and also the line $y = \hat{a} + \hat{b}x$ found in the solution to Example 4. Write down the gradients of the two lines.

5.7 Spearman's rank correlation coefficient

In certain investigations a rank is more appropriate than a measure. For example, if you were testing brands of cola you might feel that you could put them in order of taste preference but would not care to allocate marks. This kind of investigation is common in psychology and it was a psychologist, Charles Spearman (1863 – 1945), who first developed a coefficient of correlation between rankings. The derivation of this coefficient is covered on the next tasksheet.

TASKSHEET 4E – *A beauty contest*

> Suppose that n candidates are ranked in two different ways. If d_i is the difference in the rankings for the ith candidate, then the Spearman rank correlation coefficient is
>
> $$r_s = 1 - \frac{6 \sum d_i^2}{n(n^2 - 1)}$$
>
> As with the product moment coefficient, $-1 \le r_s \le 1$.
>
> $r_s \approx 1$ when the rankings are in close agreement.
> $r_s \approx -1$ when the rankings differ greatly.

Example 5

In a competition two judges ranked ten pianists as follows.

Competitor	1	2	3	4	5	6	7	8	9	10
Ranks { Judge A	10	4	5	2	1	8	9	6	7	3
Judge B	9	1	5	3	2	7	10	4	8	6
Difference in ranks	1	3	0	–1	–1	1	–1	2	–1	–3

How well do the two judges agree?

Solution

$$r_s = 1 - \frac{6 \times 28}{10 \times 99} = 0.83$$

The high positive value of r_s implies close agreement between the judges.

Exercise 4

1. At a flower show nine roses are ranked for quality and size of bloom, as follows.

Rose		1	2	3	4	5	6	7	8	9
Rank	quality	8	3	1	9	4	2	7	5	6
	size	3	5	6	7	8	4	9	1	2

   Calculate the value of r_s. Are the rankings in general agreement?

2. In Example 5, take the rankings of Judges A and B as being marks x and y, respectively. Calculate the product moment coefficient r for the two sets of marks and compare it with the rank coefficient r_s.

3. Twelve students took a test. After a refresher course they took a further test. The results were as follows.

Student	1	2	3	4	5	6	7	8	9	10	11	12
First mark, x	30	75	58	34	52	70	50	81	62	35	57	60
Second mark, y	22	59	78	50	41	71	32	60	49	40	55	61

   (a) Calculate the product moment correlation coefficient r.

   (b) Rank the marks x and the marks y.

   (c) Calculate the rank correlation coefficient r_s.

   (d) Comment on your answers to (a) and (c).

After working through this chapter you should be able to

1. explain the term 'bivariate distribution';

2. calculate Pearson's product moment correlation coefficient r and interpret its value;

3. understand the difference between correlation and causation;

4. fit least squares regression lines and use them for prediction;

5. calculate Spearman's rank correlation coefficient r_s and interpret its value.

Covariance

1. Draw scatter plots for each of the samples P, Q and R. By inspection of the graphs, comment on the correlation between X and Y in each case.

Sample P		Sample Q		Sample R	
X	Y	X	Y	X	Y
17	8.4	13	7.7	24	3.5
19	8.6	14	6.1	28	4.5
20	7.8	17	9.2	31	2.8
22	7.2	18	7.9	33	2.9
25	7.1	18	10.4	34	3.4
26	6.1	18	11.3	35	2.0
28	6.5	21	11.7	35	5.0
29	5.8	22	13.0	38	3.8
31	5.4	22	14.9	41	4.4
33	4.8	23	13.9	43	2.9
33	4.2	26	14.8	48	4.3
35	4.8	26	15.8	49	3.5

The object of this tasksheet is to investigate a measure for correlation. The method you will use considers the distribution of the points of a scatter plot with respect to new axes through the central point $(\bar{x}, \bar{y})$.

The diagram shows the scatter plot for a sample of positively correlated variables. Question 2 refers to this diagram.

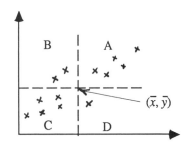

2. (a) In which of the quadrants A, B, C, D do most the points lie?

    (b) If a point (x, y) is in quadrant A, what is the sign of

        (i) $x - \bar{x}$ (the 'moment about the new y-axis')
        (ii) $y - \bar{y}$ (the 'moment about the new x-axis')
        (iii) $(x - \bar{x})(y - \bar{y})$ (the 'product moment')?

    Now answer the same questions (i), (ii) and (iii) when (x, y) lies in quadrants B, C, D respectively.

    (c) Explain why $\sum_{i} (x_i - \bar{x})(y_i - \bar{y})$ is a measure of correlation.

(continued)

65

3.   For each of the samples P, Q and R, find $\bar{x}, \bar{y}$ and, on the scatter plot, draw axes parallel to the original axes through the point $(\bar{x}, \bar{y})$.

4.   In each of the three cases calculate $\sum\limits_{i} (x_i - \bar{x})(y_i - \bar{y})$ and explain the significance of the three results.

5.   The statistic normally used is the **covariance**, defined by

$$\text{Cov}(X, Y) = \frac{1}{n} \sum\limits_{i} (x_i - \bar{x})(y_i - \bar{y})$$

Why do you think the factor $\frac{1}{n}$ is introduced?

Moderating exam marks

At the end of the GCSE mathematics course in a school, the moderator looks at the internally marked coursework and adjusts the marks to ensure an even standard amongst schools. The moderator cannot look at every pupil's work so asks for a sample of size 10 covering the range of marks achieved. The moderator adjusts the marks for the 10 pupils with the following results.

Teacher's mark	Moderator's adjusted mark
X	Y
15	27
24	36
34	37
43	48
47	47
56	52
60	65
70	66
83	70
90	80

1.   Draw a scatter plot of the data.

2.   Find the product moment coefficient r and comment on the correlation between X and Y.

3.   Estimating by eye, draw the straight line which seems best to model the data. Can you think of a particular point through which the line should pass? If so, calculate the coordinates of the point and find whether your estimated line passes through it.

4.   Use your line to predict the moderated mark for a pupil whose mark from the teacher was 20.

5.   On the basis of your model, what teacher's mark is most likely if the moderated mark is 56?

Estimating exam marks

The questions in this tasksheet refer to the situation described in Tasksheet 2. The table is repeated for your convenience.

Teacher's mark	Moderator's adjusted mark
X	Y
15	27
24	36
34	37
43	48
47	47
56	52
60	65
70	66
83	70
90	80

You should already have calculated r for these data and the value $r = 0.98$ is needed for the following calculations.

1.   If the line of best fit for regression of y on x has equation $y = \hat{a} + \hat{b}x$, calculate $\hat{a}$ and $\hat{b}$.

2.   Draw the line of best fit on the scatter plot for the data.

Now check the results you obtained 'by eye' in answering Tasksheet 2. In each case show your working from the equation and verify your answer from your graph.

3.   Use your line to predict the moderated mark for a pupil whose mark from the teacher was 20.

4.   On the basis of your model what teacher's mark is most likely if the moderated mark is 56?

A beauty contest

In a 'beautiful poodle' competition there are eight competitors and two judges A and B. Each judge assigns a ranking to the competitors as follows.

Poodle	1	2	3	4	5	6	7	8
Rank $\{$ A (x)	4	7	1	5	2	3	8	6
B (y)	8	4	3	7	5	1	6	2
Difference	–4	3	–2	–2	–3	2	2	4

1. Explain why the sum of the differences is zero.

2. For each judge in turn find the mean and variance of the rank numbers.

3. Now generalise: if there were n dogs instead of 8, what would be the mean and variance?

4. Still in the general case, use the result $\displaystyle\sum_{i=1}^{n} i^2 = \frac{1}{6} n (n+1)(2n+1)$ to show that

$$\sum_{i=1}^{n} d_i^{\,2} = \frac{1}{3} n (n+1)(2n+1) - 2 \sum_{i=1}^{n} x_i y_i$$

5. In the particular case quoted with 8 dogs, find the covariance of the rankings and the product moment coefficient r.

6. Show that in the general case, with n dogs, $\displaystyle r = 1 - \frac{6\sum d_i^{\,2}}{n(n^2-1)}$

7. What value does r take when the judges

    (a) agree exactly in their rankings   (b) disagree totally?

[The last answer is not unexpected but not easy to prove.
The result $1.2 + 2.3 + 3.4 + \ldots + (n-1)n = \frac{1}{3} n(n^2-1)$ may be useful.]

1. To assess the **reliability** of an examination it is often compared with one which has already been accepted and may be regarded as 'standard'. A new test and a standard test were given to the same group of 20 students and the following sets of marks were obtained.

new (x)	60	53	43	31	53	58	68	40	43	70
standard (y)	46	53	56	47	57	54	71	29	57	75

new (x)	86	85	50	45	51	68	30	15	50	68
standard (y)	76	87	58	36	40	53	32	24	48	66

   (a) Find (i) the product moment and (ii) the rank correlation coefficients.

   (b) Comment on the reliability of the new test as indicated by the two coefficients.

2. Collect data on the heights and weights of a sample of people of various ages (say the brothers and sisters of members of your group). Let X be the set of heights in cm, Y the set of weights in kg. Find the product moment coefficient between

   (a) X and Y (b) X^3 and Y.

   Comment on your findings.

3. In an experiment the reaction time of a subject was measured at various temperatures. These results were obtained.

temp t (°C)	2.6	5.0	7.5	9.3	12.6	15.2	19.0	21.2	23.5	25.2	27.3
Time r (ms)	48	40	26	21	20	21	19	24	28	38	50

   The researcher calculated the product moment coefficient and noted:

   '$r \approx 0$, so temperatures and reaction times are unrelated.'

   Check the accuracy of the researcher's calculation, then draw a scatter plot of the data and present an alternative conclusion.

4. Collect data on the ages (x, in years, to the nearest tenth) and heights (y, in cm, to the nearest cm) of a sample of 20 growing girls.

   (a) Find the equation of the regression line of y on x and use it to estimate the height of a girl exactly 10.0 years old.

   (b) Could you use your equation to estimate the height of a 20 year old woman?

SOLUTIONS

1 *Hypothesis testing*

1.2 The null hypothesis

State whether you think the null and alternative hypotheses for this experiment should be

$$H_0 : p = \frac{1}{2} \qquad\qquad H_0 : p = \frac{1}{2}$$

$$\text{OR}$$

$$H_1 : p > \frac{1}{2} \qquad\qquad H_1 : p \neq \frac{1}{2}$$

where p is the probability that she makes a correct identification. Justify your answer.

His friend claims to be able to 'taste the difference'. If she had none correct, she would have identified every one incorrectly. She could still claim to be able to 'taste the difference'; she simply did not know which was which. The correct alternative hypothesis in this case is $H_1 : p \neq \frac{1}{2}$.

1.3 Making the wrong decision

(a) Calculate the probability of a type I error if H_0 is rejected for $X > 10$.

(b) Explain why it is not possible to calculate the probability of a type II error.

(c) What would be the probability of a type I error if H_0 is rejected for $X > 9$?

(d) If it is decided to reject H_0 for $X > 9$ rather than $X > 10$, will the probability of a type II error increase or decrease?

(e) The farmer and his friend agree that a probability of 5% for a type I error is reasonable. For what x is $P(X > x) = 0.05$?

(a) $P(X > 10) = P\left(Z > \frac{10 - 6.2}{1.8}\right)$
$= P(Z > 2.111)$
≈ 0.0174

(b) The probability of a type II error is $P\left(Z < \frac{10 - \mu}{1.8}\right)$
You cannot evaluate this unless you know μ.

(c) $P(X > 9) \approx P(Z > 1.556) \approx 0.060$

(d) The probability of a type II error will decrease.

(e) $P(Z > 1.645) = 0.05$ so $\frac{x - 6.2}{1.8} = 1.645 \Rightarrow x = 9.161$

1.4 Level of significance

> **Draw similar diagrams to show the critical regions of a Normal distribution for one and two-tail tests when the level of significance is**
>
> **(a)   1%**   **(b)   0.1%**

(a)

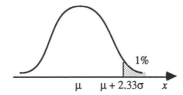   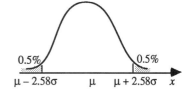

(b)

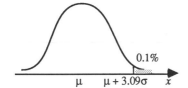   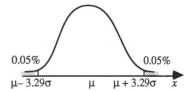

> **Has there been a 'highly significant' increase in her support?**

$$P(R \geq 75) \approx P(X > 74.5) = P(Z > \frac{74.5 - 60}{6}) = 0.0044$$

This falls in the 'very significant' 1% region, but **not** in the 'highly significant' 0.1% region.

Exercise 1

1. $H_0 : p = \frac{1}{5}$
      $H_1 : p > \frac{1}{5}$
      Level of significance: 5%

   If $R \sim B(120, \frac{1}{5})$ then the Normal approximation is $X \sim N(24, 19.2)$.
   The critical region is $X > 24 + 1.645 \sqrt{19.2}$ or $X > 31.2$.

   H_0 is rejected for $R \geq 32$. A candidate is unlikely to be answering purely by guesswork if he/she obtains 32 or more correct answers.

2. The null hypothesis is that the probability that a digit is even is $\frac{1}{2}$.

$H_0 : p = \frac{1}{2}$

$H_1 : p \neq \frac{1}{2}$

Level of significance: 5%

If R is the number of even digits out of fourteen, then $R \sim B(14, \frac{1}{2})$.

The data give $R = 4$. This is clearly not in the upper critical region but could be in the lower critical region.

$P(R \leq 4) \approx 0.09$. This is greater than $2\frac{1}{2}\%$ and so H_0 is **not** rejected.

3. $H_0 : \mu = 1300$
$H_1 : \mu < 1300$

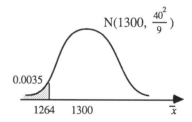

The data give $\bar{x} = 1264$
$P(\bar{X} < 1264) = P(Z < -2.7)$
≈ 0.0035

This is significant at the 1% level but not the 0.1% level. There is very significant evidence that the breaking strain is lower than expected.

4. If the machine is out of adjustment then the mean can be either too large or too small, so a two tail test is appropriate.

$H_0 : \mu = 3.00$

$H_1 : \mu \neq 3.00$

Level of significance: 5%

As $3.01 < 3.014$, $\bar{x} = 3.01$ is **not** in the critical region therefore H_0 is not rejected at the 5% level of significance. The machine does not need adjusting.

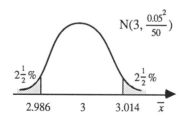

5. $H_0 : \mu = 0.85$

$H_1 : \mu > 0.85$

$$P(\bar{X} > 0.91) = P\left(Z > \frac{0.91 - 0.85}{\sqrt{(\frac{0.04}{60})}}\right)$$

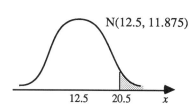

$$= P(Z > 2.324)$$

$$\approx 0.0101$$

The result is in the 'significant' 5% critical region but not quite in the 'very significant' 1% critical region. The evidence would therefore be described as 'significant'. (You should note that the sample mean, $\bar{x} = 0.91$, has probably been rounded. A more accurate value could be used and the evidence might then become 'very significant'.)

6. If p is the probability that a patient experiences side-effects, then

$H_0 : p = 0.05$
$H_1 : p > 0.05$
Level of significance: 1%

$X \sim N(12.5, 11.875)$ is the Normal approximation to $R \sim B(250, 0.05)$

$$P(R \geq 21) = P\left(Z > \frac{20.5 - 12.5}{\sqrt{(11.875)}}\right)$$

$$= P(Z > 2.322)$$

$$\approx 0.0102$$

As $P(R \geq 21)$ is greater than 1%, the result is **not** 'very significant' so H_0 is not rejected. You should note that the Normal approximation is just an approximation. A more accurate calculation based on the binomial distribution could have rejected H_0, but you would find this very difficult to calculate as few (if any) calculators can evaluate an expression such as $\frac{250!}{13! \, 237!} \, 0.05^{13} \, 0.95^{237}$.

7. (a)

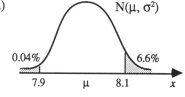

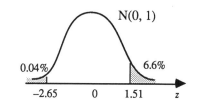

$$\left.\begin{array}{l} \mu = 8.1 - 1.51\sigma \\ \mu = 7.9 + 2.65\sigma \end{array}\right\} \qquad \begin{array}{l} \mu = 8.0274 \\ \sigma = 0.04808 \end{array}$$

(b)

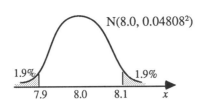

N(8.0, 0.04808²)

1.9% 1.9%

7.9 8.0 8.1 x

$$P(X < 7.9) = P(X > 8.1) = P(Z > \frac{8.1 - 8.0}{0.04808})$$

$$= P(Z > 2.08)$$

$$= 0.0188 \ (\approx 1.9\%)$$

About 3.8% of rods will be wasted.

(c) $H_0 : \mu = 8.0$

$H_1 : \mu \neq 8.0$

Level of significance: 5%

As $\bar{x} = 8.02$ mm does not lie in the critical region, H_0 is not rejected. The evidence does not suggest that the machine needs readjusting.

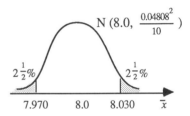

$N(8.0, \frac{0.04808^2}{10})$

$2\frac{1}{2}\%$ $2\frac{1}{2}\%$

7.970 8.0 8.030 $\bar{x}$

1.5 Population proportions

> **Support for the Liberal party is approximately 20%. What size of sample is needed to predict support for this party to within 3% with 95% certainty?**

$$1.96 \sqrt{\left(\frac{0.2 \times 0.8}{n}\right)} \approx 0.03$$

$$n \approx 683$$

Exercise 2

1. $H_0 : p = 0.46$

$H_1 : p > 0.46$

Level of significance: 5%

$$z = \frac{P_s - p}{\sqrt{\left(\frac{p(1-p)}{n}\right)}} \approx \frac{0.06}{\sqrt{\left(\frac{0.46 \times 0.54}{400}\right)}} \approx 2.41$$

$2.41 > 1.645$ and so H_0 is rejected. There is significance evidence that there has been an increase in the Labour vote.

he discrepancy is not significant .

here is significance evidence that the
rtion of people who prefer their product.

2   *Student t-distribution*

2.2   Small samples

> When $\upsilon = 8$ and $p = 0.025$, you can see from the table that $t = 2.31$.
>
> (a)   Draw a diagram to show this information.
>
> (b)   Explain carefully what this information tells you about the distribution of sample means.
>
> (c)   Look at the last line in the table. Explain how (and why) these values relate to the corresponding points on the standard Normal distribution.

(a)

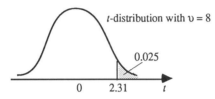

(b)   If $X \sim N(\mu, \sigma)$ and $t = \frac{\bar{x}-\mu}{(s_{n-1}/\sqrt{9})}$ where x and s_{n-1} are calculated from a random sample of 9 x-values, then $P(T > 2.31) = 0.025$.

(c)   These values are precisely the same as the values of z where $Z \sim N(0, 1)$. This suggests that a t-distribution with $\upsilon = \infty$ is a standard Normal distribution.

Exercise 1

1.   (a)   If $n = 6$ then $\upsilon = 5$. From the table, $t = 3.36$ for $p = 0.01$

   (b)   If $n = 15$ then $\upsilon = 14$. From the table, $t = 2.14$ for $p = 0.025$.

2. $H_0 : \mu = 0$
   $H_1 : \mu \neq 0$
   Level of significance: 10%

   For the sample, $\bar{x} = 21.5$, $s_{n-1} = 51.32$ and $n = 10$.

   $$t = \frac{21.5 - 0}{(51.32 / \sqrt{10})} = 1.32$$

   Accept H_0 as $1.32 < 1.83$. The evidence for a difference in times is not significant at the 10% level.

3.　$H_0 : \mu = 1000$

　　$H_1 : \mu < 1000$

　　Level of significance: 5%

　　As the sample size is large, assume that $T \sim N(0, 1)$.

$$t = \frac{997 - 1000}{(13 / \sqrt{200})} = -3.26$$

As $-3.26 < -1.645$, you should reject H_0 in favour of H_1. (As the sample size is **very** large, the test is very sensitive and although the result is undoubtedly significant, an average shortfall of 3 hours in the life of a battery is unlikely to produce a storm of protest!)

2.3　Confidence intervals

(a)　Show how this inequality can be rearranged to give:

$$\bar{x} - 2.2 \left(\frac{s_{n-1}}{\sqrt{12}}\right) < \mu < \bar{x} + 2.2 \left(\frac{s_{n-1}}{\sqrt{12}}\right)$$

(b)　Calculate s_{n-1} for the sample of frogs.

(c)　Hence show that the 95% confidence interval for the mean weight of the population of frogs is : $87.7 < \mu < 128.1$.

(d)　Calculate the 90% confidence interval.

(a)　Looking at each part of the inequality separately gives

$$-2.2 < \frac{\bar{x} - \mu}{(s_{n-1} / \sqrt{12})} \quad \text{and} \quad \frac{\bar{x} - \mu}{(s_{n-1} / \sqrt{12})} < 2.2$$

$$\Rightarrow -2.2 \left(\frac{s_{n-1}}{\sqrt{12}}\right) < \bar{x} - \mu \quad \text{and} \quad \bar{x} - \mu < 2.2 \left(\frac{s_{n-1}}{\sqrt{12}}\right)$$

$$\Rightarrow \mu < \bar{x} + 2.2 \left(\frac{s_{n-1}}{\sqrt{12}}\right) \quad \text{and} \quad \bar{x} - 2.2 \left(\frac{s_{n-1}}{\sqrt{12}}\right) < \mu$$

$$\Rightarrow \bar{x} - 2.2 \left(\frac{s_{n-1}}{\sqrt{12}}\right) < \mu < \bar{x} + 2.2 \left(\frac{s_{n-1}}{\sqrt{12}}\right)$$

(b)　$s_{n-1} = 31.80$

(c) $107.9 - 2.2 \times \dfrac{31.8}{\sqrt{12}} < \mu < 107.9 + 2.2 \times \dfrac{31.8}{\sqrt{12}}$

$\Rightarrow 87.7 < \mu < 128.1$

The 95% confidence interval is (87.7, 128.1).

(d)   The 90% confidence interval is $(107.9 - 1.795 \times \dfrac{31.8}{\sqrt{12}},\ 107.9 + 1.795 \times \dfrac{31.8}{\sqrt{12}})$, which is (91.4, 124.4).

Note that the table does not show critical t-values for $\upsilon = 11$ and so you have to estimate the value knowing that the critical value is 1.81 for $\upsilon = 10$ and 1.78 for $\upsilon = 12$. A good estimate for $\upsilon = 11$ is therefore $(1.81 + 1.78) \div 2 = 1.795$.

Exercise 2

1.   If x is the weight of a peach, assume that $X \sim N(\mu, \sigma^2)$.

(a)   For the sample, $\bar{x} = 132$ and $s_{n-1} = 18.6$. As the sample size is $n = 10$, the number of degrees of freedom is $\upsilon = 9$.

The 90% confidence interval for μ is

$$(132 - 1.83 \times \dfrac{18.6}{\sqrt{10}},\ 132 + 1.83 \times \dfrac{18.6}{\sqrt{10}}) = (121.2,\ 142.8)$$

(b)   The 95% confidence interval for μ is

$$(132 - 2.26 \times \dfrac{18.6}{\sqrt{10}},\ 132 + 2.26 \times \dfrac{18.6}{\sqrt{10}}) = (118.7,\ 145.3)$$

The 99% confidence interval for μ is

$$(132 - 3.25 \times \dfrac{18.6}{\sqrt{10}},\ 132 + 3.25 \times \dfrac{18.6}{\sqrt{10}}) = (112.9,\ 151.1)$$

2.   Assume that $X \sim N(\mu_x, \sigma_x^2)$ and that $Y \sim N(\mu_y, \sigma_y^2)$

For each sample, $n = 15$ and so the resulting t-distribution will have $\upsilon = 14$ degrees of freedom.

For the sample without alcohol: $\bar{x} = 11.7$ and $s_{n-1} = 2.05$.

The 95% confidence interval for μ_x is

$$(11.7 - 2.14 \times \dfrac{2.05}{\sqrt{15}},\ 11.7 + 2.14 \times \dfrac{2.05}{\sqrt{15}}) = (10.6,\ 12.8)$$

For the sample with alcohol: $\bar{y} = 17.1$ and $s_{n-1} = 4.97$

The 95% confidence interval for μ_y is

$$(17.1 - 2.14 \times \dfrac{4.97}{\sqrt{15}},\ 17.1 + 2.14 \times \dfrac{4.97}{\sqrt{15}}) = (14.4,\ 19.8)$$

As the confidence intervals do not overlap it is very unlikely that $\mu_x = \mu_y$. The alcohol does appear to have slowed down the second group.

2.4 Matched pairs *t*-test

> (a) Calculate $\bar{x}$ and s_{n-1} for the sample of weight changes, and use a *t*-test to show that the sample does not provide significant evidence in support of the manufacturer's claim.
>
> (b) Does this prove that the manufacturer's claim is false?

(a) $\bar{x} = -0.5,\ s_{n-1} = 0.852$

$$t = \frac{\bar{x} - \mu}{(s_{n-1}/\sqrt{8})} \text{ has a } t\text{-distribution with } \upsilon = 7$$

$$t = \frac{-0.5 - 0}{(0.852/\sqrt{8})} = -1.66$$

As $-1.66 > -1.89$, you should **not** reject H_0.

(b) No. The probability of accepting H_0 when H_1 is in fact true can be quite large, especially if the mean decrease in weight, μ, is small.

Exercise 3

1. If X is the difference in corrosion ('uncoated' – 'coated'), then assume that $X \sim N(\mu, \sigma^2)$.

$H_0 : \mu = 0$
$H_1 : \mu > 0$
Level of significance: 1%

$$t = \frac{\bar{x} - \mu}{(s_{n-1}/\sqrt{9})} \text{ will have a } t\text{-distribution with } \upsilon = 8.$$

The sample gives x: 16, 12, –4, –1, –2, 6, 20, 3, 12

Then $\bar{x} = 6.89,\ s_{n-1} = 8.54$ and $t = \dfrac{6.89 - 0}{8.54/3} = 2.42$

As $2.42 < 2.90$, you should not reject H_0. The sample does not provide very significant evidence in support of the manufacturer's claim.

2. If X is the improvement in score, then assume that $X \sim N(\mu, \sigma^2)$

$H_0 : \mu = 0$
$H_1 : \mu > 0$
Level of significance: 5%

$$t = \frac{\bar{x} - \mu}{(s_{n-1}/\sqrt{15})} \text{ will have a } t\text{-distribution with } \upsilon = 14.$$

The sample gives x : 1, –1, 1, 3, –1, 2, 3, 4, 1, –1, 4, 3, 1, 0, 3

Then $\bar{x} = 1.53$, $s_{n-1} = 1.77$ and $t = \dfrac{1.53 - 0}{1.77 / \sqrt{15}} = 3.35$.

As $3.35 > 1.76$, H_0 is rejected in favour of H_1. The sample provides significant evidence to support the claim that the course of instruction improves recall.

3.   If D kg is the difference in weight loss, then assume that $D \sim N(\mu, \sigma^2)$.

$H_0 : \mu = 0$

$H_1 : \mu \neq 0$

Level of significance: 5%

D :   3, 1, 0, 3, 1, –2, 4, –1, 1, – 4

Then $\bar{x} = 0.6$, $s_{n-1} \approx 2.46$ and $t = \dfrac{0.6}{2.46 / \sqrt{10}} \approx 0.77$ with $\upsilon = 9$.

As $0.77 < 2.26$, you should not reject H_0. The evidence of weight loss is not significant at the 5% level.

3 *Two sample tests*

3.1   Comparing two means

> Suppose ten representatives, who travel large distances,
> were asked to use the new petrol while ten office staff who
> just drive to and from work each weekday were asked to
> use four-star. Why would this not be a valid trial?

Even when using the same fuel for both trials, rates of consumption for long and short
distance journeys are not equal.

> (a)   What are the probability distributions for the populations
>   of sample means $\bar{X}$ and $\bar{Y}$?
>
> (b)   Calculate $\bar{x}$ and $\bar{y}$ for the sample data.   Check that $\bar{x} > \bar{y}$.
>   If not, it is not worth continuing the test!

(a) $\bar{X} \sim N\left(\mu_X,\ \frac{1.8^2}{10}\right)$, $\bar{Y} \sim N\left(\mu_Y,\ \frac{1.8^2}{10}\right)$

(b) $\bar{x} = 34.37$, $\bar{y} = 32.99$

3.2   Testing the equality of two means

> Find P(Z > 1.71).

$1 - 0.9564 = 0.0436$

> Find P(Z < − 2.15)

$1 - 0.9842 = 0.0158$

Exercise 1

1. H_0 : The average age at which men in countries A and B first marry is the same; $\mu_A = \mu_B$.

    H_1 : On average, men marry later in life in country B than in country A; $\mu_A < \mu_B$.

    A 1% one-tail test is to be applied. H_0 is to be rejected if $z < -2.33$.

    $$\bar{A} - \bar{B} \sim N\left(\mu_A - \mu_B, \frac{\sigma_A^2}{80} + \frac{\sigma_B^2}{100}\right)$$

    The test statistic is $z = \dfrac{\bar{a} - \bar{b}}{\sqrt{\left(\dfrac{\sigma_A^2}{80} + \dfrac{\sigma_B^2}{100}\right)}}$

    Substituting $\bar{a} = 24.5$, $\bar{b} = 2.61$, $\sigma_A^2 = 3.2^2$, $\sigma_B^2 = 2.8^2$

    $$z = \frac{-1.6}{0.45} = -3.5$$

    H_0 is rejected in favour of H_1; there is strong evidence that men marry later in country B than in country A.

2. Let the population of annual costs be £X for the first model and £Y for the second model.

    H_0 : Cars of both models have the same average maintenance costs; $\mu_X = \mu_Y$.

    H_1 : The second model is more expensive to maintain than the first; $\mu_X < \mu_Y$.

    A 5% one-tail test is to be applied. H_0 is to be rejected if $z < -1.645$.

    $$\bar{X} - \bar{Y} \sim N\left(\mu_X - \mu_Y, \frac{\sigma_X^2}{20} + \frac{\sigma_Y^2}{11}\right)$$

    The test statistic is $z = \dfrac{\bar{x} - \bar{y}}{\sqrt{\left(\dfrac{\sigma_X^2}{20} + \dfrac{\sigma_Y^2}{11}\right)}}$

    Substituting $\bar{x} = 540$, $\bar{y} = 710$, $\sigma_X^2 = 90^2$, $\sigma_Y^2 = 110^2$

    $$z = \frac{-170}{38.8} = -4.38$$

    Since $-4.38 < -1.645$, H_0 is rejected in favour of H_1. The company should be advised to use only the first model.

    There is no evidence that the parent populations are Normally distributed and, for such small samples, the assumption that the sample means are Normally distributed is not justified. Nevertheless, as a result of the test the company would probably phase out the use of the second model.

3. $H_0 : \mu_B = \mu_G$

$H_1 : \mu_B > \mu_G$

The test is 1% one-tail. H_0 is to be rejected if $z > 2.33$.

$$z = \frac{7.1}{\sqrt{(\frac{144}{50} + \frac{196}{50})}} = 2.72$$

H_0 is rejected. Assuming that the mean levels of capability in logical thinking of boys and girls are equal, there is strong evidence that the test is biased in favour of boys.

4. $H_0 : \mu_X = \mu_Y$

$H_1 : \mu_X \neq \mu_Y$

The test is 5% two-tail. H_0 is to be rejected if $z < -1.96$ or $z > 1.96$.

$$z = \frac{1.5}{\sqrt{(\frac{16}{50} + \frac{16}{50})}} = 1.875$$

H_0 is accepted. There is no significant change in mean length.

5. $H_0 : \mu_U = \mu_O$

$H_1 : \mu_U < \mu_O$

The test is 5% one-tail. H_0 is to be rejected if $z < -1.645$.

$$\bar{u} = 7.96, \quad \bar{o} = 10.66$$

$$z = \frac{-2.70}{\sqrt{(\frac{1.20^2}{12} + \frac{1.41^2}{10})}} = -4.78$$

H_0 is rejected.

3.3   Confidence intervals

> (a)   Use the above result to find a 95% confidence interval for $\mu_X - \mu_Y$ in Example 3.
>
> (b)   Find a 99% confidence interval for $\mu_X - \mu_Y$.

(a) $\bar{x} - \bar{y} \pm 1.96 \sqrt{(\frac{8500}{100} + \frac{8500}{98})} = -28 \pm 25.7$

The 95% confidence interval is $(-53.7, -2.3)$.

(b) $-28 \pm 2.575 \sqrt{(\frac{8500}{100} + \frac{8500}{98})} = -28 \pm 33.8$

The 99% confidence interval is $(-61.8, 5.8)$.

Exercise 2

1.   Let the distributions be $X \sim N(10.3, 25)$ and $Y \sim N(8.2, 36)$.

$(10.3 - 8.2) \pm 1.96 \sqrt{(\frac{25}{50} + \frac{36}{72})} = 2.10 \pm 1.96$

The 95% confidence interval is $(0.14, 4.06)$.

2. $-2.70 \pm 1.96 \sqrt{(\frac{1.2^2}{12} + \frac{1.41^2}{10})} = -2.70 \pm 0.62$

The required interval is $(-3.32, -2.08)$.

3. $1.38 \pm 1.645 \sqrt{(\frac{1.8^2}{10} + \frac{1.8^2}{10})} = 1.38 \pm 1.32$.

The required interval is $(0.06, 2.70)$.

4.   Assume that the tar content in mg of brand A is $X \sim N(9.9, 1.6^2)$ and that the tar content in mg of brand B is $Y \sim N(8.9, 1.6^2)$. Then,

$$1 \pm 2.575 \sqrt{(\frac{1.6^2}{100} + \frac{1.6^2}{100})} = 1 \pm 0.58$$

The required interval is $(0.42, 1.58)$.

3.4   Pooled variance estimator

> (a)   **Find the mean and variance, s_A^2, of the times for A**
>
> (b)   **Find the mean and variance, s_B^2, of the times for B.**

(a)   Mean = 68.4, $s_A^2 \approx 253.31$

(b)   Mean = 83.42, $s_B^2 \approx 285.08$

> **Explain the above derivation of the pooled variance estimator.**

The distribution of $\frac{15}{14} s_A^2$ has mean σ^2 and so the distribution of $15 s_A^2$ has mean $14 \sigma^2$. Similarly, the distribution of $12 s_B^2$ has mean $11 \sigma^2$ and so $15 s_A^2 + 12 s_B^2$ has mean $14 \sigma^2 + 11 \sigma^2 = 25 \sigma^2$.

$\dfrac{15 s_A^2 + 12 s_B^2}{25}$ is therefore an unbiased estimator for σ^2.

(a) For the samples of times for treatments A and B given earlier, find three separate unbiased estimators for the population variance using

(i) sample A only;

(ii) sample B only;

(iii) a pooled estimator.

(b) Explain why the three estimates are different. In what sense is the pooled estimate likely to be the 'best' of the three estimates?

(a) (i) $\frac{15}{14} s_A^2 \approx 271.6$

(ii) $\frac{12}{11} s_B^2 \approx 311.0$

(iii) $\dfrac{15 s_A^2 + 12 s_B^2}{25} \approx 288.8$

(b) Each estimator has its own distribution. All three estimates are unbiased and so the three distributions all have mean σ^2.

The values given in (a) simply represent individual points in each distribution and cannot therefore be expected to be the same. Because the pooled estimate uses more data, its distribution can be expected to be more closely grouped around σ^2 and therefore any particular pooled estimate is likely to be close to σ^2.

3.5 Two sample t-test

Complete the significance test for the two treatments. Carefully state your conclusion.

The pooled variance estimator is 288.82

$$t = \frac{68.40 - 83.42}{\sqrt{288.82}\,\sqrt{(\frac{1}{15} + \frac{1}{12})}} \approx -2.28, \ \upsilon = 25$$

H_0 is rejected in favour of H_1. There is significant evidence that drug A is more effective.

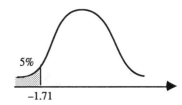

5%

−1.71

Exercise 3

1.   (a) $\dfrac{6 \times 1.2 + 8 \times 1.7}{6 + 8 - 2} \approx 1.73 \text{ kg}^2$

    (b) $H_0 : \mu_A = \mu_B$

         $H_1 : \mu_A \neq \mu_B$

         Level of significance: 5%

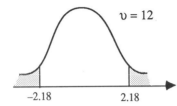

$$ t = \dfrac{3.3 - 4.1}{\sqrt{1.73}\ \sqrt{(\frac{1}{6} + \frac{1}{8})}} \approx -1.13 $$

         There is no significant difference between the mean weight losses.

2.   (a) $\bar{a} = 26.775$ $s_A^2 \approx 0.307$ $n_A = 4$

         $\bar{b} = 25.55$ $s_B^2 \approx 0.629$ $n_B = 6$

         A pooled estimate of variance is $\dfrac{4 \times 0.307 + 6 \times 0.629}{4 + 6 - 2} \approx 0.625$

    (b) $H_0 : \mu_A = \mu_B$

         $H_1 : \mu_A > \mu_B$

         Level of significance: 5%

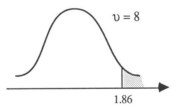

$$ t = \dfrac{26.775 - 25.55}{\sqrt{0.625}\ \sqrt{(\frac{1}{4} + \frac{1}{6})}} \approx 2.40 $$

         At the 5% level, H_0 should be rejected in favour of H_1. There is significant evidence that trout from the Arn have a greater average length than those from the Bate.

3. $H_0 : \mu_1 = \mu_2$

$H_1 : \mu_1 \neq \mu_2$

Level of significance: 5%

$\overline{x}_1 = 3.1 \qquad s_1^2 = 0.275 \qquad n_1 = 4$

$\overline{x}_2 = 3.5 \qquad s_2^2 = 0.093 \qquad n_2 = 6$

A pooled estimate of variance is $\dfrac{4 \times 0.275 + 6 \times 0.093}{4 + 6 - 2} \approx 0.2075$

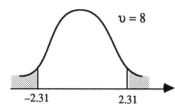

$t = \dfrac{-0.4}{\sqrt{0.2075} \ \sqrt{(\frac{1}{4} + \frac{1}{6})}} \approx -1.36$

The difference between the means of the two samples is not significant.

4. $H_0 : \mu_A = \mu_J$

$H_1 : \mu_A \neq \mu_J$

$\overline{a} = 2.148 \qquad s_A^2 \approx 0.00206 \qquad n_A = 5$

$\overline{j} = 2.084 \qquad s_J^2 \approx 0.00134 \qquad n_J = 7$

A pooled estimate of variance is $\dfrac{5 \times 0.00206 + 7 \times 0.00134}{5 + 7 - 2} \approx 0.00197$

$t = \dfrac{2.148 - 2.084}{\sqrt{0.00197} \ \sqrt{(\frac{1}{5} + \frac{1}{7})}} \approx 2.5$

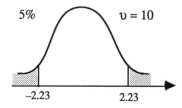
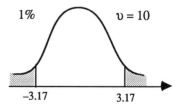

The evidence for a difference in playing ability is significant at 5% but not at 1%.

4 *Non-parametric tests*

4.1 The sign test

Exercise 1

1. H_0 : median = 1.82

   H_1 : median $\neq$ 1.82

   Level of significance: 5%

   The data give:

   $-\ -\ +\ +\ -\ -\ +\ +\ +\ -\ -\ +\ +\ +\ +\ -\ +\ +\ +\ -$ $(r = 12)$

   If $R \sim B(20, \frac{1}{2})$, then, using a program, $P(R \geq 12) \approx 0.252$ (25.2%).

   As 25.2% > 2.5%, $r = 12$ is not in the critical region and H_0 is not rejected in favour of H_1. There is no significant difference from the findings of the Gallup Polls.

2. H_0 : median = 28

   H_1 : median $\neq$ 28

   Level of significance: 5%

   The data give:

   $-\ -\ -\ -\ -\ -\ -\ -\ -\ -\ 0\ +\ +\ +$ $(r = 3)$

   If $R \sim B(13, \frac{1}{2})$ then $P(R \leq 3) = \left[\binom{13}{0} + \binom{13}{1} + \binom{13}{2} + \binom{13}{3} \right] \left(\frac{1}{2} \right)^{13}$

   $$= 0.046 \quad (4.6\%)$$

   As 4.6% > 2.5%, $r = 3$ is not in the critical region and H_0 is not rejected. (Had this been a one-tail test, then H_0 would have been rejected.) The locusts bred in captivity can be assumed to have a median lifetime of 28 days.

3. H_0 : median improvement = 0

   H_1 : median improvement > 0

   Level of significance: 5%

   The data give:

   $+\ 0\ +\ +\ -\ +\ +\ +\ +\ +$ $(r = 8)$

   If $R \sim B(9, \frac{1}{2})$ then $P(R \geq 8) = \left[\binom{9}{8} + \binom{9}{9} \right] \left(\frac{1}{2} \right)^{9} = 0.020 \quad (2\%)$

   As 2% < 5%, $R = 8$ is in the critical region and so H_0 is rejected in favour of H_1. There is significant evidence to support the maker's claim.

4.2   The Wilcoxon signed-rank test

> **What has to be assumed about the population distribution for a two sample t-test?**

You must assume that the parent populations are both Normal and have the same variance.

> **Find the sum of the ranks corresponding to negative differences.**

$2.5 + 2.5 + 4 + 6 + 6 + 6 + 8.5 + 8.5 + 12 + 13 = 69$

> (a)   Explain how you would expect the size of T to provide evidence for or against the null hypothesis.
>
> (b)   Complete the hypothesis test for the locusts.

(a)   If the null hypothesis is true you would expect the sum of ranks corresponding to positive differences to be roughly equal to the sum corresponding to negative differences. If the null hypothesis is false you would expect the sums to differ substantially. Therefore, the smaller the value of T the stronger will be the evidence for rejecting the null hypothesis.

(b)   From the table of critical values for the Wilcoxon signed-rank test, the critical value is 17.

$T > 17$ and so H_0 is accepted. The locusts bred in captivity can be assumed to have a median lifetime of 28 days.

Exercise 2

1. H_0 : median $= 24$
      H_1 : median > 24
      Level of significance: 5%

Difference	−1	3	4	−4	2	2	0	−7	14	0	9	15
Rank	1	4	5.5	5.5	2.5	2.5	–	7	9	–	8	10

$T = 1 + 5.5 + 7 = 13.5$ $n = 10$

The critical value is 10 and so H_0 is accepted. The data do not provide significant evidence that the median is greater than 24.

2. H_0 : median = 60

H_1 : median < 60

Level of significance: 5%

Differences	−12	10	−42	−40	−7	−13	16
Rank	3	2	7	6	1	4	5

$T = 2 + 5 = 7$. For $n = 7$, the critical value at the 5% level is 3 and so the evidence for a lower median score is not significant.

3. H_0 : median = 0

H_1 : median ≠ 0

Level of significance: 5%

Differences	8	3	2	4	6	5	6	7	−1	−4
Rank	10	3	2	4.5	7.5	6	7.5	9	1	4.5

$T = 1 + 4.5 = 5.5$.

For $n = 10$, the critical value at the 5% level for a two-tail test is 8 and so there is significant evidence for a difference in time.

5 Correlation and regression

5.1 Bivariate distributions

> What do the 2's on the plot signify?

For each '2' on the plot there are two pairs of identical data.

5.2 The product moment correlation coefficient

> What happens to Cov (X, Y) if all the values of X are multiplied by 5 and all the values of Y by 4?

The sample covariance will be multiplied by a scale factor of $5 \times 4 = 20$.

> What happens to r if all the values of X are multiplied by 5 and all the values of Y by 4?

r is unchanged, since $s_x\, s_Y$ is increased by the same scale factor as Cov (X, Y). Note also that r is a pure nunber; the dimensions in which X and Y are measured cancel out in the expression for r.

> Explain why (a) $\sum \bar{x}\bar{y} = n\bar{x}\bar{y}$, (b) $\bar{y}\sum x_i = n\bar{x}\bar{y}$

(a) $\sum \bar{x}\bar{y} = \bar{x}\bar{y} + \bar{x}\bar{y} + ... + \bar{x}\bar{y} = n\bar{x}\bar{y}$

(b) Since $\dfrac{1}{n}\sum x_i = \bar{x}$, $\sum x_i = n\bar{x}$

Exercise 1

1. (a) –

   (b) $r = 0.989$. The temperatures are strongly correlated.

2. For both sets $r = -1$.

   Both sets of points lie exactly on straight lines with negative gradients of –2 and – 4 respectively.

3. (a) $r = 0.646$.

    (b) $r > 0$ but is not very close to 1. The correlation is not strong.

4. (a) $r = 0.991$.

    (b) –

    (c) Despite the high value of r, as you can check, the relationship between l and T is not linear. You should find that the relationship between l and T^2 is almost linear.

5.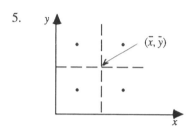

    $r = 0$.
    The points are at the four corners of a square.
    The diagram shows why the covariance is zero.

6E. (a) $a^2 + b^2 - 2ab = (a - b)^2 \geq 0$
    $\Rightarrow a^2 + b^2 \geq 2ab$

    (b) (i) $(x_1^2 + x_2^2)(y_1^2 + y_2^2) - (x_1 y_1 + x_2 y_2)^2$

    $= x_1^2 y_2^2 + x_2^2 y_1^2 - 2x_1 x_2 y_1 y_2$

    $= (x_1 y_2 - x_2 y_1)^2 \geq 0$

    Hence the required result.

    (ii) $(x_1^2 + x_2^2 + x_3^2)(y_1^2 + y_2^2 + y_3^2) - (x_1 y_1 + x_2 y_2 + x_3 y_3)^2$

    $= \quad x_1^2 y_2^2 + x_2^2 y_1^2 - 2x_1 x_2 y_1 y_2$

    $+ x_1^2 y_3^2 + x_3^2 y_1^2 - 2x_1 x_3 y_1 y_3$

    $+ x_2^2 y_3^2 + x_3^2 y_2^2 - 2x_2 x_3 y_2 y_3$

    $= (x_1 y_2 - x_2 y_1)^2 + (x_1 y_3 - x_3 y_1)^2 + (x_2 y_3 - x_3 y_2)^2 \geq 0$

    (c) In general, $\sum x_i^2 \sum y_i^2 \geq \left(\sum x_i y_i \right)^2$

    Similarly,

    $$\sum (x_i - \bar{x})^2 \sum (y_i - \bar{y})^2 \geq \left[\sum (x_i - \bar{x})(y_i - \bar{y}) \right]^2$$

    which establishes the result that

    $$[\text{Cov}(X, Y)]^2 \leq s_X^2 s_Y^2.$$

Then $\qquad r^2 = \dfrac{[\text{Cov}(X, Y)]^2}{s_X^2 s_Y^2} \leq 1$

$$\Rightarrow -1 \leq r \leq 1$$

5.3 Correlation and causation

> (a) In which of the three categories would you place the connection between weight and height?
>
> (b) In the 1980's there was a steady increase in the student population of Sheffield. In the same town, there was also a steady increase in cases of thefts of cars. Into which of the categories above would you place this example?

(a) In general, you would expect tall people to have a relatively heavy bone structure and to weigh more than short people. You would therefore expect a positive correlation between height and weight.

Height and weight both depend upon the genetic make-up and early nutrition of the individual. However, weight can be independently changed by diet and lifestyle. The relationship is therefore described by a combination of the second and third categories.

(b) Without further evidence the example would be placed in the third category; the increases appear causally unrelated. It is possible that the same changes in society have caused both increases and then the example would fall into the second category.

5.4 A line of best fit

> Why would it not be sensible to try to minimise $\displaystyle\sum_{1}^{n} d_i$?

If the values of d_i were simply added together the positive and negative values would tend to cancel each other out.

5.5 Equation of a line of best fit

Exercise 2

1. (a) $r = -0.955$ so there is a strong negative correlation between Y and X.

   (b) –

(c) $y = 819.4 - 2.66x$

(d)   –

(e)   When $x = 95$, $y = 819.4 - (2.66 \times 95) = 567$

(f) $x = 60$ is outside the range of validity of the trial. It is possible that the reaction time is not being governed by the heart rate but by some other effect of the drug. Other ways of affecting the heart rate, such as exercise, might be tried instead of the drug.

2.   (a) $r = 0.902$.

(b) $y = -1.634 + 0.276x$

(c)   The yield increases slowly until about 25 g of fertiliser is used, then more rapidly. Two different lines for the ranges $10 \le x \le 25$ and $25 < x \le 32$ would provide a better model.

5.6   Regressing X on Y

Exercise 3

1.   The equation of the regression line of X on Y is

$$x = 0.024y - 0.108$$

The gradients are respectively $\hat{b} = 37.6$ and $\frac{1}{\hat{d}} = 41.6$ Both lines pass through $(\bar{x}, \bar{y})$ and therefore the two lines are in close agreement for values of x near to $\bar{x}$.

5.7   Spearman's rank correlation coefficient

Exercise 4

1.

Quality	8	3	1	9	4	2	7	5	6
Size	3	5	6	7	8	4	9	1	2
Difference	5	-2	-5	2	-4	-2	-2	4	4

$$r_s = 1 - \frac{6 \times 114}{9 \times 80} = 0.05$$

The rankings do not show general agreement.

2. $r = r_s = 0.83$. Spearman's rank correlation coefficient is simply the product moment correlation coefficient applied to rankings.

3. (a) $r = 0.669$

(b)
x rank	12	2	6	11	8	3	9	1	4	10	7	5
y rank	12	5	1	7	9	2	11	4	8	10	6	3
Difference	0	-3	5	4	-1	1	-2	-3	-4	0	1	2

(c) $r_s = 1 - \dfrac{6 \times 86}{12 \times 143} = 0.699$

(d) Although very similar, the coefficients are not the same. As seen in question 2, if rankings are taken as scores then $r = r_s$. If rankings are found from given scores, then generally $r \neq r_s$.

COMMENTARIES

1 Hypothesis testing

1.1 Making a decision

> **(a)** What is the probability that a die is classified as 'loaded' when in fact it is 'fair'?
>
> **(b)** What is the probability that a die is classified as 'fair' when in fact it is 'loaded'?
>
> **(c)** Do you think the teacher should change her threshold for rejecting a die as 'fair' from fourteen to
>
>   **(i)** thirteen   **(ii)** fifteen   **(iii)** some other value?
>
> Justify your answer.
>
> **(d)** Suppose a die showed a six on just two occasions. How would you interpret such a result?

(a) If the die is 'fair', the number of sixes out of sixty, $R \sim B(60, \frac{1}{6})$.
The Normal approximation is $X \sim N(10, 8\frac{1}{3})$.

$$P(R \geq 14) \approx P(X > 13.5)$$
$$\approx P\left(Z > \frac{13.5 - 10}{\sqrt{8\frac{1}{3}}}\right)$$
$$\approx P(Z > 1.212)$$
$$\approx 0.113$$

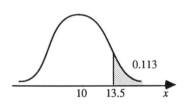

There is a probability of 0.113 that a fair die will be wrongly classified as 'loaded'.

(b) If the die is 'loaded', the number of sixes out of sixty, $R \sim B(60, \frac{1}{4})$.
The Normal approximation is $X \sim N(15, 11\frac{1}{4})$.

$$P(R < 14) \approx P(X < 13.5)$$
$$\approx P\left(Z < \frac{13.5 - 15}{\sqrt{11\frac{1}{4}}}\right)$$
$$\approx P(Z < -0.447)$$
$$\approx 0.327$$

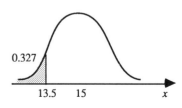

There is a probability of 0.327 that a biased die will be wrongly accepted as 'fair'.

(c) (i)

Fair die
$X \sim N(10, 8\frac{1}{3})$

Probability of a wrong decision

12.5

$$z = \frac{12.5 - 10}{\sqrt{(8\frac{1}{3})}} = 0.866$$

$P(Z > 0.866) = 0.193$

The probability of wrongly classifying a fair die as 'loaded' is
$P(Z > 0.866) \approx 0.193$

The probability of wrongly classifying a loaded die as 'fair' is
$P(Z < -0.745) \approx 0.229$

(ii) The probability of wrongly classifying the die 'loaded' $\approx P(Z > 1.559) \approx 0.059$

The probability of wrongly classifying the die 'fair' $\approx P(Z < -0.149) \approx 0.440$

What is the 'best' threshold is open to discussion.

(d) Although it would be very unlikely that a number as low as (or lower than) this might occur, it is possible. It is unlikely to happen if the die is 'fair', but it is even more unlikely to happen with a 'loaded' die, so you should conclude that the die is 'fair'.

The binomial distribution

1. (a) You should find that the probability is approximately 0.115.
   (b) You should find that the probability is approximately 0.33.

2. If the probability of obtaining precisely 14 sixes is 0.115, then you might expect 14 sixes to occur 200 x 0.115 = 23 times if you repeat the experiment 200 times. However, the number of times 14 sixes occurs in 200 repetitions of the experiment is itself a random variable and can take any value from 0 to 200. Although 23 would be the 'expected' value, any number from 14 to 32 would not be considered unusual. You should therefore find your estimate of the probability to be between 0.07 and 0.16 each time you repeat the simulation.

   For similar reasons you would expect your answer to question 1(b) to vary each time you carry out the simulation.

3. You should find that the probability is approximately 0.12.

4. $P(R = 14) = \frac{60!}{14!\,46!} \times 0.25^{14} \times 0.75^{\,46} = 0.11565783 \ldots$

   See the commentary to question 2 for an explanation as to why the values obtained in question 1(a) might vary from 0.07 to 0.16.

5. Mean = 60 x 0.25 = 15
   Variance = 60 x 0.25 x 0.75 = 11.25

6. $P(R = 14) \approx P(13.5 < X < 14.5)$
   Therefore $P(R > 14) \approx P(X > 14.5)$ and $P(R \geq 14) \approx P(X > 13.5)$ as it **includes** $P(R = 14)$.

7. (a) $R \sim B(60, \frac{1}{6})$ has mean 10 and variance $8\frac{1}{3}$.
   $$P(R \geq 14) \approx P\left(Z > \frac{13.5 - 10}{\sqrt{8\frac{1}{3}}} \right)$$
   $$\approx 0.113$$

   (b) $R \sim B(60, \frac{1}{4})$ has mean 15 and variance $11\frac{1}{4}$.
   $$P(R < 14) \approx P\left(Z < \frac{13.5 - 15}{\sqrt{11\frac{1}{4}}} \right)$$
   $$\approx 0.327$$

8. (a) $P(R \geq 14) = 0.115216 \ldots$ (b) $P(R < 14) = 0.334911 \ldots$

9. (a) You would not expect your answers to questions 1 and 3 to be precisely equal to your answers to question 8 for reasons similar to those given in the commentary to question 2.

   (b) The method used in question 7 gives an approximation, whereas the method used in question 8 gives an accurate answer.

1. $H_0 : P = 0.22$

     $H_1 : P > 0.22$

     Level of significance: 5%

     $R \sim B(80, 0.22)$ is approximated by $X \sim N(17.6, 13.728)$

     $P(R \geq 24) \approx P(X > 23.5) > 5\%$ and so $r = 24$ is not included in the critical region.

     Reject H_0 if $R \geq 25$

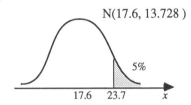

N(17.6, 13.728)

5%

17.6   23.7   x

As the data gave $r = 25$, H_0 is rejected. Support does appear to be significantly higher than the national average.

2.   (a) $H_0 : \mu = 1000$

            $H_1 : \mu > 1000$

            Level of significance: 5%

            The mean production over 100 days has distribution N $(1000, \frac{20^2}{100})$.

$$z = \frac{1006 - 1000}{20/10} = 3$$

            $3 > 1.645$ and so the improvement is significant at the 5% level.

     (b)   (i)   A type I error is a rejection of H_0 when it is true. This would mean the consultants receiving an additional fee even though there has not been an improvement in production.

$$z = \frac{1003.3 - 1000}{20/10} = 1.65 \text{ and so the probability of a type I error is}$$

                  approximately 5%, the significance level of the test.

           (ii)   A type II error is the acceptance of H_0 when it is false. This would mean the consultants not receiving an additional fee even though there has been an improvement in production.

$$z = \frac{1003.3 - 1004}{20/10} = -0.35$$

                  $P(Z < -0.35) = 1 - \Phi (0.35) \approx 0.3632$

                  The probability of a type II error in this case is approximately 36%.

2 Student t-distribution

2.1 Large samples

> Before using organic methods, a gardener kept detailed records and found that his cucumbers had a mean length of 35.0 cm. To check the lengths of his organically grown cucumbers, he takes a random sample of 100 and measures their lengths. He finds that the sample mean is $x = 34.1$ cm and that $s_{n-1}^2 = 16.0$ cm^2.
>
> Does this constitute evidence of a decrease in length? State carefully any assumptions you make.

- Assume that s_{n-1}^2 is a good estimate of the population variance i.e. that $\sigma^2 = 16.0$.
- Assume that $X \sim N(35, \frac{16}{100})$.

$H_0 : \mu = 35$

$H_1 : \mu < 35$

Level of significance: 5%

$$z = \frac{\bar{x} - \mu}{\sigma / \sqrt{n}} = \frac{34.1 - 35}{\sqrt{(16/100)}} = -2.25$$

H_0 is rejected because $-2.25 < -1.645$. There is significant evidence to support the claim that organic cucumbers are shorter.

Note

Because of the Central Limit Theorem, it is reasonable to assume that

$$\frac{\bar{X} - \mu}{\sigma / \sqrt{n}} \sim N(0, 1)$$

Similarly, you know that s_{n-1} is an unbiased estimator of σ. However, a particular value of s_{n-1} might differ considerably from σ. As you will see in this chapter, the distribution of $\frac{\bar{X} - \mu}{S_{n-1}/\sqrt{n}}$ is **not** Normally distributed, although the difference is small for **large n.**

Student t-distribution

1. $x : 62, 63.5, 65, 62.5$

    $\bar{x} = 63.25, s_{n-1}^2 = 1.75, \mu = 65.535$

    $$t = \frac{63.25 - 65.535}{\sqrt{(1.75/4)}} = -3.455$$

2. (a) $z = \dfrac{63.25 - 65.535}{\sqrt{(6.540/4)}} = -1.787$

    (b) $\bar{X} \sim N(\mu, \frac{\sigma^2}{n}) \Rightarrow \bar{X} - \mu \sim N(0, \frac{\sigma^2}{n})$

    $$\Rightarrow Z \sim N(0, 1)$$

3. Replacing the constant, σ^2, by a random variable S_{n-1}^2 adds 'uncertainty' to the distribution so you might expect the distribution of T to be more 'spread out' (i.e. have a greater variance) than a standard Normal distribution.

4. You would not expect so many values with magnitude greater than 2 in a standard Normal distribution. The general shape, although still 'bell-shaped', is narrower around the peak and more spread out in the tails.

5. (a) Substituting $\upsilon = 3$, you obtain

    $$c_3 \left(1 + \frac{t^2}{3}\right)^{-\frac{(3+1)}{2}} = c_3 \left(1 + \frac{t^2}{3}\right)^{-2}$$

    (b) A sketch of the function shows that the area under the graph for $|t| > 10$ is negligible. A numerical method such as the mid-ordinate rule shows that:

    $$\int_{-10}^{10} \left(1 + \frac{t^2}{3}\right)^{-2} dt \approx 2.715 \quad \text{(4 s.f.)}$$

(continued)

105

(c) $\displaystyle\int_{-\infty}^{\infty} f(t)\,dt = 1 \Rightarrow \int_{-\infty}^{\infty} c_3\left(1+\dfrac{t^2}{3}\right)^{-2} dt = 1$

$\Rightarrow c_3 = 1 \div \displaystyle\int_{-\infty}^{\infty}\left(1+\dfrac{t^2}{3}\right)^{-2} dt$

$\approx 1 \div 2.715$

$\approx 0.368 \quad (3 \text{ s.f.})$

6E. The author's graphic calculator gave the following results.

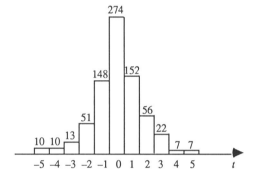

This compares very well with that obtained by Student.

1. (a) A sketch of the function on a graph plotter suggests that the area under the graph for $|t| > 10$ is negligible. A numerical method for integration such as the mid-ordinate rule shows that

$$\int_{-10}^{10} \left(1 + \frac{t^2}{5}\right)^{-3} dt \approx 2.634 \quad \text{(4 s.f.)}$$

   (b) When $\upsilon = 5$, $f(t) = c_5 \left(1 + \frac{t^2}{5}\right)^{-3}$

   So $\displaystyle\int_{-\infty}^{\infty} f(t)\, dt = 1 \Rightarrow c_5 \int_{-\infty}^{\infty} \left(1 + \frac{t^2}{5}\right)^{-3} dt = 1$

   $\Rightarrow c_5 \approx \dfrac{1}{2.634} \approx 0.380$

   (c) $c_{10} \approx 0.390$
   $c_{20} \approx 0.394$
   $c_{50} \approx 0.397$

2. (a) (i) $\upsilon = 3$; $f(t) = 0.368 \left(1 + \frac{t^2}{3}\right)^{-2}$ \quad (see Tasksheet 1)

   (ii) $\upsilon = 5$; $f(t) = 0.380 \left(1 + \frac{t^2}{5}\right)^{-3}$

   (iii) $\upsilon = 10$; $f(t) = 0.390 \left(1 + \frac{t^2}{10}\right)^{-5.5}$

   (iv) $\upsilon = 20$; $f(t) = 0.394 \left(1 + \frac{t^2}{20}\right)^{-10.5}$

   (v) $\upsilon = 50$; $f(t) = 0.397 \left(1 + \frac{t^2}{50}\right)^{-25.5}$

   (b)(c) –

   (d) You should find that the graph of the *t*-distribution approaches that of a standard Normal distribution as the value of υ (the degrees of freedom) increases. The graphs are virtually indistinguishable when $\upsilon = 50$.

   This implies that the random variable $\quad T = \dfrac{\overline{X} - \mu}{\left(\dfrac{S_{n-1}}{\sqrt{n}}\right)}$

   can be assumed to have N(0, 1) distribution for $n > 50$. In practice, the Normal approximation to the *t*-distribution is often used for a sample size $n \geq 30$.

1. Assume that the random variable from which the sample is drawn is $X \sim N(\mu, \sigma^2)$.

$H_0 : \mu = 6.5$

$H_1 : \mu \neq 6.5$

Level of significance: 5%

$t = \dfrac{\bar{x} - \mu}{s_{n-1}/\sqrt{n}}$ has a *t*-distribution

with $\upsilon = n - 1$ degrees of freedom.

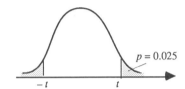

$p = 0.025$

For the sample: $\bar{x} = 6.71$ and $s_{n-1} = 0.68$, so $t = \dfrac{6.71 - 6.5}{0.68/\sqrt{n}}$

(a) $n = 10 \Rightarrow \upsilon = 9$, $t = 0.977 < 2.26$: Not significant

(b) $n = 25 \Rightarrow \upsilon = 24$, $t = 1.544 < 2.06$: Not significant

(c) $n = 50 \Rightarrow \upsilon = 49$, $t = 2.184 > 2.01$: Significant

(d) $n = 100 \Rightarrow \upsilon = 99$, $t = 3.088 > 1.98$: Significant

The last result is in fact very significant (i.e. significant at the 1% level) as the critical value is 2.63. However, it is not highly significant.

2. Assume that if X is the weight of a potato, then $\bar{X} \sim N(\mu, \frac{\sigma^2}{\sqrt{n}})$. This is a reasonable assumption because the sample size is large.

From the sample: $\bar{x} = 145.3$, $s_{n-1} = 87.9$ and $n = 60$.

The statistic $t = \dfrac{\bar{x} - \mu}{s_{n-1}/\sqrt{n}}$

will have a *t*-distribution with

$\upsilon = 59$ degrees of freedom.

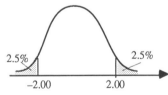

2.5% 2.5%

−2.00 2.00

The 95% confidence interval for the mean, μ, is

$(145.3 - 2.00 \times \frac{87.9}{\sqrt{60}}, \; 145.3 + 2.00 \times \frac{87.9}{\sqrt{60}}) = (122.6, 168.0)$

Had you used the Normal approximation to the *t*-distribution as the sample size is ≥ 30, you would have obtained a slightly narrower interval. It is important to remember that the Normal distribution is an **approximation** to the *t*-distribution. It is **not** equal to it just because $n \geq 30$.

(continued)

3.   Assume that if X is the length of the component, then $X \sim N(\mu, \sigma^2)$.

From the sample: $\bar{x} = 30.04$, $s_{n-1} = 0.050$ and $n = 8$.

The statistic $t = \dfrac{\bar{x} - \mu}{s_{n-1}/\sqrt{n}}$ has a t-distribution with $\upsilon = 7$ degrees of freedom.

The 95% confidence interval for the mean, μ, is

$$\left(30.04 - 2.36 \times \tfrac{0.050}{\sqrt{8}}, \ 30.04 + 2.36 \times \tfrac{0.050}{\sqrt{8}}\right) = (30.00, 30.08)$$

The confidence interval only just includes the nominal mean. Had you conducted a hypothesis test:

$H_0 : \mu = 30.0$

$H_1 : \mu \neq 30.1$

Level of significance: 5%

then you would **not** have rejected H_0 as the calculated value of t would have been just inside the region of acceptance.

4.   If 87% are satisfactory, then 13% are not.

$H_0 : p = 0.13$

$H_1 : p > 0.13$

Level of significance : 5%

If R is the number of unsatisfactory chips out of a sample of 15, then $R \sim B(15, 0.13)$.

$P(R \geq 4) = 12.0\%$ (3 s.f.)

As $12\% > 5\%$, do not reject H_0. The sample does **not** provide significant evidence that the unit's output has deteriorated.

This problem is based on a small sample size ($n = 15$) but has **nothing** to do with the t-distribution. Although the Normal approximation to the binomial is valid for large samples, it is **incorrect** to use the t-distribution as an approximation to the binomial for small samples!

3   *Two sample tests*

3.1   Comparing two means

You will need the program *Ncomb*.

The variables used in the program are X and Y where

$$X \sim N(\mu_X, \sigma_X{}^2) \text{ and } Y \sim N(\mu_Y, \sigma_Y{}^2)$$

The computer generates 300 values of a selected combination of X and Y and plots the results on a histogram together with the sample mean and variance.

(a)   **Input values of μ_X, μ_Y, $\sigma_X{}^2$, $\sigma_Y{}^2$ of your own choice and investigate the distribution of $X - Y$.**

(b)   **Repeat (a) several times, using different means and variances for X and Y.**

(c)   **In your opinion, is the distribution of $X - Y$ Normal? Explain your answer.**

(d)   **How are the mean and variance of $X - Y$ related to the means and variances of X and Y?**

(a,b)   In each case you should find that the distribution of $X - Y$ is roughly bell-shaped.

(c)   The distribution is, in fact, Normal. You may have considered some of the following features.

- The distribution is roughly symmetric.

- In a Normal distribution, about 68% of the population is within one standard deviation of the mean.

- In a Normal distribution, about 95% of the population is within two standard deviations of the mean.

(d)   Mean of $X - Y = \mu_X - \mu_Y$

Variance of $X - Y = \sigma^2{}_X + \sigma^2{}_Y$

1. (a) $H_0 : \mu_A = \mu_B$

   $H_1 : \mu_A < \mu_B$

   In a one-tail test, H_0 will be rejected with

   95% certainty if $z < -1.645$
   99% certainty if $z < -2.33$

   It is reasonable to assume that $\overline{A} - \overline{B} \sim N(\mu_A - \mu_B, \frac{10.8}{50} + \frac{10.8}{50})$

   Then $z = \dfrac{42.8 - 43.9}{\sqrt{(\frac{10.8}{50} + \frac{10.8}{50})}} \approx -1.67$

   H_0 is rejected in favour of H_1 at the 5% but not at the 1% level. There is evidence that A is a harder marker than B but it is not very strong.

   (b) With 98% confidence, $\mu_A - \mu_B = -1.1 \pm 2.33 \sqrt{(\frac{21.6}{50})}$

   $$= -1.10 \pm 1.53$$

   The required interval is $(-2.63, 0.43)$.

2. Let W be the population of lengths in mm of eggs laid in the nests of wrens and D be the corresponding population for hedge sparrows (dunnocks). To apply the test it must be assumed that

   $$\overline{W} - \overline{D} \sim N(\mu_W - \mu_D, \frac{\sigma^2}{15} + \frac{\sigma^2}{14})$$

   $H_0 : \mu_W = \mu_D$

   $H_1 : \mu_W < \mu_D$

   Level of significance: 5%

   For the samples, $\overline{w} = 21.25$ $\quad s_W^2 = 0.481$

   $\overline{d} = 23.11$ $\quad s_D^2 = 1.023$

(continued)

The pooled variance estimate for σ^2 is

$$\frac{15 \times 0.481 + 14 \times 1.023}{15 + 14 - 2} \approx 0.798$$

Then $t = \dfrac{21.25 - 23.11}{\sqrt{0.798}\ \sqrt{(\frac{1}{15} + \frac{1}{14})}} \approx -5.60$

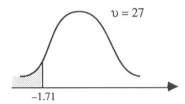

$\upsilon = 27$

-1.71

At the 5% level, H_0 is rejected in favour of H_1.

There must be considerable doubt concerning the pooled variance which was estimated from small samples having very different variances. Nevertheless, there is strong evidence that cuckoos adapt to their host species by laying larger eggs in dunnocks' than in wrens' nests.

4 Non-parametric tests

4.1 The sign test

> **(a)** If r is the number of plus signs, why is it reasonable for her to assume that $R \sim B(36, \frac{1}{2})$?
>
> **(b)** Does her sample provide significant evidence in support of the alternative hypothesis?
>
> **(c)** In theory, why is there zero probability that a gap is precisely equal to the median value?
>
> **(d)** In practice, why are you likely to find that some data items are equal to the median?

(a) The median divides a probability distribution into two equal areas, each equal to a half.

$$P(T > 4.8) = P(T < 4.8) = \frac{1}{2}.$$

Therefore, under H_0, the plus signs occur with probability $\frac{1}{2}$. As there are 36 'trials' when a plus sign can occur, $R \sim B(36, \frac{1}{2})$.

(b) The data give $r = 22$.

For $R \sim B(36, \frac{1}{2})$, you must calculate $P(R \geq 22)$. Using one of the programs for binomial probabilities that were introduced in Chapter 1, you should find that $P(R \geq 22) \approx 0.12$. As $P(R \geq 22)$ is greater than $2\frac{1}{2}\%$, the result is not significant and H_0 is not rejected.

(c) If the probability density function of T is f(t), then $P(T = 4.8) = \int_{4.8}^{4.8} f(t)\, dt = 0$

(d) In practice, data items are measured to a specified degree of accuracy. If data items are measured to one decimal place accuracy, then the data item $T = 4.8$ would have an actual value $4.75 \leq T < 4.85$,

and $P(4.75 \leq T < 4.85) = \int_{4.75}^{4.85} f(t)\, dt \neq 0$

Tutorial sheet

1.   (a) H_0 : median = 100

        H_1 : median > 100

        Level of significance: 5%

        The data give: $+ + - - + + + +$ $(r = 6)$

        If $R \sim B(8, \frac{1}{2})$ then $P(R \geq 6) = \left[\binom{8}{6} + \binom{8}{7} + \binom{8}{8} \right] \left(\frac{1}{2} \right)^8 = 0.145$

        $r = 6$ is **not** in the critical region so H_0 is **not** rejected at the 5% level of significance.

    (b) $H_0 : \mu = 100$

        $H_1 : \mu > 100$

        Level of significance: 5%

        Reject H_0 if $\overline{X} > 108.72$

        The data give $\overline{x} = 109.875$

        As $x > 108.72$, H_0 **is** rejected.

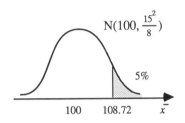

    (c)   The sign test is less powerful than the test based on the Normal distribution. This means that while both tests have the same probability of a type I error (5%), the sign test has a greater probability of a type II error. You should always use a significance test based on the probability distribution of the data when it is known.

2.   (a) H_0 : median = 120

        H_1 : median > 120

    (b)   (i) $+ + + - + + + - + + + -$ $(r = 9)$

              $R \sim B(12, \frac{1}{2})$. $P(R \geq 9) = \left[\binom{12}{9} + \binom{12}{10} + \binom{12}{11} + \binom{12}{12} \right] \left(\frac{1}{2} \right)^{10} \approx 0.073$

              The manufacturer's claim is accepted at the 5% level.

        (ii)

Difference	10	20	40	−20	30	60	50	−40	20	70	40	−30
Rank	1	3	8	3	5.5	11	10	8	3	12	8	5.5

              $T = 3 + 8 + 5.5 = 16.5$

              From the table for $n = 12$, the 5% critical value for a one-tail test is 17. The manufacturer's claim is therefore rejected at the 5% level.

    (c)   As seen in question 1, the sign test has a relatively high probability of giving a type II error.

5 Correlation and regression

5.1   Bivariate distributions

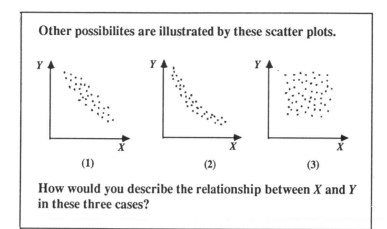

Other possibilites are illustrated by these scatter plots.

(1)   (2)   (3)

How would you describe the relationship between X and Y in these three cases?

In the case illustrated by (1) there is a strong negative correlation between X and Y. A good model for the correlation would be a linear one such as $y + x = c$.

(2) illustrates a case where there would again be a strong negative correlation. However, the best model would not be linear; possibly the relationship between X and Y is one of inverse proportionality, $X \propto \frac{1}{Y}$.

In the case illustrated by (3) there is neither positive nor negative correlation; X and Y are unrelated.

Covariance

1. From the scatter plots it should appear that:

    Sample P : there is a strong negative correlation between X and Y;
    Sample Q : there is a strong positive correlation;
    Sample R : there is little or no correlation.

2. (a) In quadrants A and C.

    (b) (i) $x - \bar{x} > 0$ (ii) $y - \bar{y} > 0$ (iii) $(x - \bar{x})(y - \bar{y}) > 0$

        For (x, y) in quadrant B the answers are:

        (i) $x - \bar{x} < 0$ (ii) $y - \bar{y} > 0$ (iii) $(x - \bar{x})(y - \bar{y}) < 0$

        If (x, y) is in quadrant C, $(x - \bar{x})(y - \bar{y}) > 0$

        If (x, y) is in quadrant D, $(x - \bar{x})(y - \bar{y}) < 0$

    (c) If X, Y are positively correlated, most points will be in quadrants A and C and $\sum (x_i - \bar{x})(y_i - \bar{y})$ will be positive.

        If X, Y are negatively correlated, most points will be in quadrants B and D and $\sum (x_i - \bar{x})(y_i - \bar{y})$ will be negative.

        If X, Y are unrelated, then points should be equally distributed in the four quadrants and $\sum (x_i - \bar{x})(y_i - \bar{y})$ will be small.

3. Values of $\bar{x}, \bar{y}$:   for P;   26.5, 6.39
                    for Q;   19.8, 11.4
                    for R;   36.6, 3.58

4. Values of $\sum (x_i - \bar{x})(y_i - \bar{y})$: for P; −93
                            for Q;   138
                            for R;   7.4

    These figures support the conclusion from the scatter plots in question 1.

5. The scaling factor $\frac{1}{n}$ ensures that covariance is not affected simply by the **size** of the sample being considered.

Moderating exam marks

1.

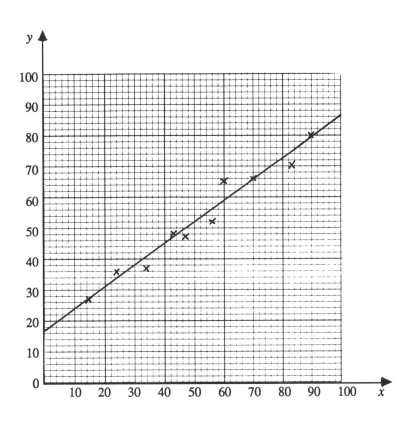

2. $r = 0.98$. There is a strong correlation between X and Y.

3.   It is likely that your line will pass close to the point $(\bar{x}, \bar{y})$. In this example, the point is
        (52.2, 52.8).

4.   You should have an estimate of approximately 31.

5.   Approximately 57.

Estimating exam marks

1. $\hat{a} = 17.17$ $\hat{b} = 0.683$

2.

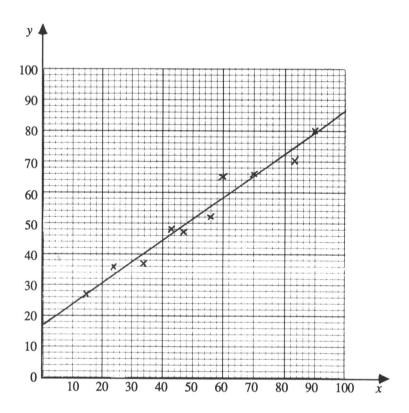

You should check that your line passes through (52.2, 52.8).

3.   The moderator's mark is estimated as $17.17 + 0.683 \times 20 \approx 31$.

4. $56 = 17.17 + 0.683 \times t$

   $\Rightarrow \quad t \approx 57$

The teacher's mark is estimated as approximately 57. Note that, according to this model, the teacher and moderator agree well in the central section of the range.

[The regression line $y = 17.17 + 0.683\, x$ is for 'Y on X' and is the best line for estimating values of Y from values of X. Theoretically, you should use the regression line for 'X on Y' for an estimate such as the one in question 4. In this example, r is approximately 1 and so the regression lines for 'Y on X' and 'X on Y' are virtually the same.]

A beauty contest

1. $\sum d = \sum (x - y)$

   $= \sum x - \sum y$

   $= 36 - 36$

2. The mean is $\frac{9}{2}$ and the variance is $\frac{21}{4}$.

3. The mean would be $\frac{1}{2}(n + 1)$

   The variance would be $\frac{1}{n} \sum_{i=1}^{n} i^2 - \left[\frac{1}{2}(n + 1) \right]^2$

   $$= \frac{1}{n} \times \frac{1}{6} n(n + 1)(2n + 1) - \frac{1}{4}(n + 1)^2$$

   $$= \frac{1}{12}(n^2 - 1)$$

4. $\sum d^2 = \sum (x - y)^2 = \sum x^2 + \sum y^2 - 2\sum xy,$ where

   $\sum x^2 = \sum y^2 = \sum_{i=1}^{n} i^2 = \frac{1}{6} n(n + 1)(2n + 1)$

   So $\quad \sum d^2 = 2 \times \frac{1}{6} n(n + 1)(2n + 1) - 2\sum xy$

   $$= \frac{1}{3} n(n + 1)(2n + 1) - 2\sum xy$$

5. $\text{Cov}(x, y) = \frac{9}{8}$, $r = 0.214$

6. $r = \dfrac{\sum xy - n\bar{x}\bar{y}}{\sqrt{\left[(\sum x^2 - n\bar{x}^2)(\sum y^2 - n\bar{y}^2) \right]}}$

   Since $\sum x^2 = \sum y^2 = \frac{1}{6} n(n + 1)(2n + 1)$ and $\bar{x} = \bar{y} = \frac{1}{2}(n + 1)$, the denominator becomes $\frac{1}{6} n(n + 1)(2n + 1) - \frac{1}{4} n(n + 1)^2 = \frac{1}{12} n(n^2 - 1)$. Substituting from the result of question 4, the numerator is

   $$\frac{1}{6} n(n + 1)(2n + 1) - \frac{1}{2}\sum d^2 - \frac{1}{4} n(n + 1)^2$$

   $$= \frac{1}{12} n(n^2 - 1) - \frac{1}{2}\sum d^2$$

(continued)

119

7.   (a)   If the judges agree totally then $d_i = 0$ for all i, so $r = 1$.

(b)   If they disagree totally then the rankings are as follows.

$$
\begin{array}{lcccccc}
X: & n & (n-1) & (n-2) & \ldots & 2 & 1 \\
Y: & 1 & 2 & 3 & \ldots & (n-1) & n \\
d: & (n-1) & (n-3) & (n-5) & \ldots & (3-n) & (1-n)
\end{array}
$$

Note that for **total** disagreement n must be even. This affords an excuse to show the calculation only in the even case! Then

$$
\begin{aligned}
\sum d^2 &= (n-1)^2 + (n-3)^2 + \ldots + (3-n)^2 + (1-n)^2 \\
&= 2\left[1^2 + 3^2 + \ldots + (n-1)^2\right] \\
&= 2\left[\sum_{i=1}^{n} i^2 - (2^2 + 4^2 + \ldots + n^2)\right] \\
&= 2\left[\sum_{i=1}^{n} i^2 - 4\sum_{i=1}^{\frac{1}{2}n} i^2\right] \\
&= \frac{1}{3}n(n+1)(2n+1) - \frac{1}{3}n(n+1)(n+2) \\
&= \frac{1}{3}n(n^2-1)
\end{aligned}
$$

and $r = 1 - \dfrac{6\sum d^2}{n(n^2-1)} = -1$

1. (a) (i) $r = 0.852$

   (ii) Ranks $\begin{cases} X & 7 \ \ 9 \ 15 \ 18 \ \ 9 \ \ 8 \ \ 4 \ 17 \ 15 \ \ 3 \ \ 1 \ \ 2 \ 12 \ 14 \ 11 \ \ 4 \ 19 \ 20 \ 12 \ \ 4 \\ Y & 15 \ 11 \ \ 9 \ 14 \ \ 7 \ 10 \ \ 4 \ 19 \ \ 7 \ \ 3 \ \ 2 \ \ 1 \ \ 6 \ 17 \ 16 \ 11 \ 18 \ 20 \ 13 \ \ 5 \end{cases}$

   $d \ \ -8 \ -2 \ \ 6 \ \ 4 \ \ 2 \ -2 \ \ 0 \ -2 \ \ 8 \ \ 0 \ -1 \ \ 1 \ \ 6 \ -3 \ -5 \ -7 \ \ 1 \ \ 0 \ -1 \ -1$

   $\sum d^2 = 320, \ \ r_s = 0.759$

   (b) Neither coefficient would inspire confidence in the new test. The low value of r_s is caused by a few major discrepancies in rank which indicate unreliability.

2. High values of r would be expected in both cases. For similar solids of uniform density, volumes and hence weights are proportional to cubes of corresponding linear dimensions (such as heights). Taking this model you would expect a higher value of r in the second case.

3. $r \approx 9 \times 10^{-3}$, so the researcher's calculation is probably correct. However, the scatter plot shows clearly that reaction times are roughly constant for 'comfortable' temperatures, in the range 8°– 20°C, say, but increase sharply as the temperature becomes uncomfortably low or high. Thus the researcher's conclusion is unjustified; a strong relation exists between reaction times and temperature, though it is not linear.

4. (a) –

   (b) The best model for increase of height with time is not linear; in human development there are 'growth spurts' at particular ages. These ages would be revealed by a survey using a large sample.

   A 20 year old woman is outside the range covered. It might be amusing to extrapolate from the regression line to find an 'expected height'. This would be considerably greater than the average height of adult females.

Programs

Binomial probabilities

You can calculate individual binomial probabilities on any scientific calculator.

For $R \sim B(n, p)$

$$P(R = r) = \binom{n}{r} p^r (1 - p)^{n-r} \text{ where } \binom{n}{r} = \frac{n!}{r!\,(n-r)!}$$

Although most scientific calculators have a factorial function, $n!$ becomes very large very quickly and if, for example your calculator cannot store numbers with a magnitude greater than 10^{100} you will find your calculator cannot evaluate $n!$ for $n > 69$. You therefore have to use the Normal approximation for samples of size 70 or more.

If you have a graphic calculator, you will find it very useful to program it to calculate $P(R \geq r)$. The following programs are written for the TEXAS TI-81 and the CASIO fx-7000GA.

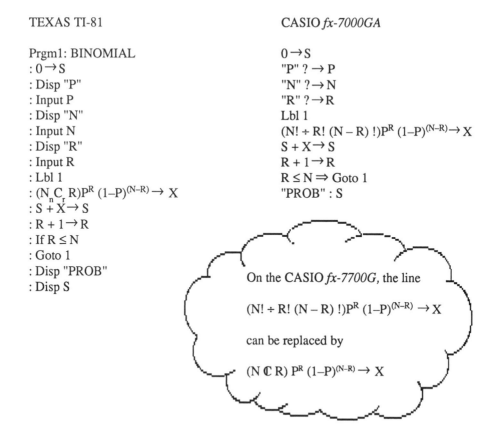

TEXAS TI-81

Prgm1: BINOMIAL
: $0 \to S$
: Disp "P"
: Input P
: Disp "N"
: Input N
: Disp "R"
: Input R
: Lbl 1
: $(_nC_r R)P^R (1-P)^{(N-R)} \to X$
: $S + X \to S$
: $R + 1 \to R$
: If $R \leq N$
: Goto 1
: Disp "PROB"
: Disp S

CASIO fx-7000GA

$0 \to S$
"P" ? $\to$ P
"N" ? $\to$ N
"R" ? $\to$ R
Lbl 1
$(N! \div R! (N-R) !)P^R (1-P)^{(N-R)} \to X$
$S + X \to S$
$R + 1 \to R$
$R \leq N \Rightarrow$ Goto 1
"PROB" : S

On the CASIO fx-7700G, the line

$(N! \div R! (N-R) !)P^R (1-P)^{(N-R)} \to X$

can be replaced by

$(N \, \mathbb{C} \, R) P^R (1-P)^{(N-R)} \to X$

The probability $P(R < r)$ can be obtained by subtracting $P(R \geq r)$ from 1. The result $P(R \geq r)$ is stored in S and so the expression 1–S will give you $P(R < r)$.

The following program replicates the original simulation carried out by 'Student' in 1908. Before you start set the range to $X_{min} = -5.5$, $X_{max} = 5.5$, $X_{scl} = 1$, $Y_{min} = 0$, $Y_{max} = 300$, $Y_{scl} = 100$. Also turn off any graphs in $\boxed{Y=}$. (N.B. The program takes 20-25 minutes to run.)

Prgm1: STUDENT	
: ClrDraw	
: ClrStat	
: 0 → V	
: −6 → T	
: Lbl 1	This clears and re-sets the statistical data.
: V + 1 → V	
: T + 1 → T	
: T → {x}(V)	
: 0 → {y} (V)	
: If V < 11	
: Goto 1	
: 0 → W	
: Lbl 2	
: W + 1 → W	This counts the number of samples generated
: If W > 750	and stops when the program reaches 750.
: Goto 5	
: Disp W	
: 4 → N	
: 0 → M	
: 0 → S	
: Lbl 3	
: 6 * Rand − 3 → X	This generates a random value of x where
: 0.4 * Rand → Y	$X \sim N(0, 1)$.
: e^ (−0.5 X²) / √(2 π) → R	
: If Y > R	
: Goto 3	
: M + X → M	
: S + X² → S	
: N − 1 → N	This calculates $\bar{x}$ and s_{n-1}^2 for each sample of
: If N > 0	four x-values and calculates the statistic t.
: Goto 3	
: M / 4 → M	
: 4 (S / 4 − M²) / 3 → S	
: M / √ (S / 4) → T	
: If T < −5	
: −5 → T	
: If T > 5	This determines the class interval for t and
: 5 → T	adds 1 to the appropriate frequency, {y} (V).
: Int (T + 6.5) → V	
: {y} (V) + 1 → {y} (V)	
: Goto 2	
: Lbl 5	This draws the final histogram. Press 'STAT EDIT
: Hist	DATA' to view the frequencies.

If you put $Y_1 = 750 * 0.368(1 + X^2 / 3) \wedge -2$ you will find that the theoretical t-distribution is superimposed when you give the command 'Hist'. (Note that the probability density function has to be multiplied by 750 to scale it up to fit the total frequency of the histogram.)

The following program replicates the original simulation carried out by 'Student' in 1908. (N.B. The program takes about 20-25 minutes to run.)

0 → V Lbl 1 V + 1 → V 0 → A[V] V< 11 ⇒ Goto 1	This assigns zero to the memories A[1] to A[11].
0 → W Lbl 2 W + 1 → W W > 750 ⇒ Goto 5	This counts the number of samples generated and stops when the program reaches 750.
4 → N 0 → M 0 → S Lbl 3 6 × Ran# –3 → X 0.4 × Ran# → Y e(–0.5 X²) ÷ √ (2 π) → R Y > R ⇒ Goto 3	This generates a random value of *x* where $X \sim N(0, 1)$.
M + X → M S + X² → S N – 1 → N N > 0 ⇒ Goto 3 M ÷ 4 → M 4 (S ÷ 4 – M²) ÷ 3 → S M ÷ √(S ÷ 4) → T	This calculates $\bar{x}$ and s_{n-1}^2 for each sample of four *x*-values and calculates the statistic *t*.
T < –5 ⇒ –5 → T T > 5 ⇒ 5 → T Int (T + 6.5) → V A[V] + 1 → A[V] Goto 2	This determines the class interval for *t* and adds 1 to the appropriate frequency A[V].
Lbl 5 0 → V Lbl 6 V + 1 → V "T" : V – 6◢ "F" : A[V]◢ V < 11 ⇒ Goto 6 "END"	This displays the values of *t* and the corresponding frequencies, *f*. (Make a note of them as they are displayed so that you can use them later.)

The values of *t* and their frequencies can now be entered as statistical data and the histogram can be plotted. (Do not forget to set the range.) You can then superimpose the graph of the theoretical *t*-distribution with $\upsilon = 3$ degrees of freedom. (Note that the probability density function has to be multiplied by 750 to scale it up to fit the total frequency of the histogram and so you should graph $Y = 750 \times 0.368 (1 + X^2 \div 3)^{-2}$.)

The following program replicates the original simulation carried out by 'Student' in 1908. (N.B. The program takes 3-4 minutes to run on a BBC B computer, but is much faster on other makes/models.)

```
10    DIM A(100)
20    FOR W=1 TO 750
30    M= 0: S=0
40    FOR N=1 TO 4
50    REPEAT
60    X=6*RND(1)–3:Y=0.4*RND(1)
70    UNTIL Y<EXP (–0.5*X^2/SQR(2*PI))
80    M=M+X:S=S+X^2
90    NEXT N
100   M=M/4
110   S=4(S/4–M^2)/3
120   T=M/SQR(S/4)
130   V=INT(T+50.5)
140   A(V)=A(V)+1
150   NEXT W
160   FOR V=40 TO 60
170   T=V–50
180   PRINT T, A(V)
190   NEXT V
```

This counts the number of samples generated.

This generates a random value of x where $X \sim N(0, 1)$ and calculates $\bar{x}$ and s_{n-1}^2 for each sample of four. It then calculates the statistic t, determines the class interval for t and adds 1 to the appropriate frequency A(V).

This prints out values of t from –10 to 10 with the observed frequencies.

The values of t and their frequencies can now be entered into a graph plotter (or graphic calculator) and the histogram can be plotted. You can then superimpose the graph of the theoretical t-distribution with $\upsilon = 3$ degrees of freedom. (Note that the probability density function has to be multiplied by 750 to scale it up to fit the total frequency of the histogram, so you should graph $Y = 750 * 0.368 (1 + T \wedge 2 / 3) \wedge – 2.$)

Tables

TABLE 1 : The standard Normal distribution

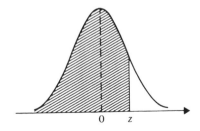

The table gives the area to the left of (or below) any given *z* value. *z* is the number of standard deviations from the mean value

z	.00	.01	.02	.03	.04	.05	.06	.07	.08	.09
.0	.5000	.5040	.5080	.5120	.5160	.5199	.5239	.5279	.5319	.5359
.1	.5398	.5438	.5478	.5517	.5557	.5596	.5636	.5675	.5714	.5753
.2	.5793	.5832	.5871	.5910	.5948	.5987	.6026	.6064	.6103	.6141
.3	.6179	.6217	.6255	.6293	.6331	.6368	.6406	.6443	.6480	.6517
.4	.6554	.6591	.6628	.6664	.6700	.6736	.6772	.6808	.6844	.6879
.5	.6915	.6950	.6985	.7019	.7054	.7088	.7123	.7157	.7190	.7224
.6	.7257	.7291	.7324	.7357	.7389	.7422	.7454	.7486	.7517	.7549
.7	.7580	.7611	.7642	.7673	.7704	.7734	.7764	.7794	.7823	.7852
.8	.7881	.7910	.7939	.7967	.7995	.8023	.8051	.8078	.8106	.8133
.9	.8159	.8186	.8212	.8238	.8264	.8289	.8315	.8340	.8365	.8389
1.0	.8413	.8438	.8461	.8485	.8508	.8531	.8554	.8577	.8599	.8621
1.1	.8643	.8665	.8686	.8708	.8729	.8749	.8770	.8790	.8810	.8830
1.2	.8849	.8869	.8888	.8907	.8925	.8944	.8962	.8980	.8997	.9015
1.3	.9032	.9049	.9066	.9082	.9099	.9115	.9131	.9147	.9162	.9177
1.4	.9192	.9207	.9222	.9236	.9251	.9265	.9279	.9292	.9306	.9319
1.5	.9332	.9345	.9357	.9370	.9382	.9394	.9406	.9418	.9429	.9441
1.6	.9452	.9463	.9474	.9484	.9495	.9505	.9515	.9525	.9535	.9545
1.7	.9554	.9564	.9573	.9582	.9591	.9599	.9608	.9616	.9625	.9633
1.8	.9641	.9649	.9656	.9664	.9671	.9678	.9686	.9693	.9699	.9706
1.9	.9713	.9719	.9726	.9732	.9738	.9744	.9750	.9756	.9761	.9767
2.0	.9772	.9778	.9783	.9788	.9793	.9798	.9803	.9808	.9812	.9817
2.1	.9821	.9826	.9830	.9834	.9838	.9842	.9846	.9850	.9854	.9857
2.2	.9861	.9864	.9868	.9871	.9875	.9878	.9881	.9884	.9887	.9890
2.3	.9893	.9896	.9898	.9901	.9904	.9906	.9909	.9911	.9913	.9916
2.4	.9918	.9920	.9922	.9925	.9927	.9929	.9931	.9932	.9934	.9936
2.5	.9938	.9940	.9941	.9943	.9945	.9946	.9948	.9949	.9951	.9952
2.6	.9953	.9955	.9956	.9957	.9959	.9960	.9961	.9962	.9963	.9964
2.7	.9965	.9966	.9967	.9968	.9969	.9970	.9971	.9972	.9973	.9974
2.8	.9974	.9975	.9976	.9977	.9977	.9978	.9979	.9979	.9980	.9981
2.9	.9981	.9982	.9982	.9983	.9984	.9984	.9985	.9985	.9986	.9986
3.0	.9987	.9987	.9987	.9988	.9988	.9989	.9989	.9989	.9990	.9990
3.1	.9990	.9991	.9991	.9991	.9992	.9992	.9992	.9992	.9993	.9993
3.2	.9993	.9993	.9994	.9994	.9994	.9994	.9994	.9995	.9995	.9995
3.3	.9995	.9995	.9995	.9996	.9996	.9996	.9996	.9996	.9996	.9997
3.4	.9997	.9997	.9997	.9997	.9997	.9997	.9997	.9997	.9997	.9998

Joint Matriculation Board

TABLE 2 : Upper percentage points for the *t*-distribution

The tabulated value is t_p, where $P(X > t_p) = p$, when X has the *t*-distribution with υ degrees of freedom.

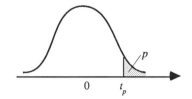

p	0.05	0.025	0.01	0.005	0.001	0.0005
$\upsilon = 1$	6.31	12.71	31.82	63.66	318.3	636.6
2	2.92	4.30	6.96	9.92	22.33	31.60
3	2.35	3.18	4.54	5.84	10.21	12.92
4	2.13	2.78	3.75	4.60	7.17	8.61
5	2.02	2.57	3.36	4.03	5.89	6.87
6	1.94	2.45	3.14	3.71	5.21	5.96
7	1.89	2.36	3.00	3.50	4.79	5.41
8	1.86	2.31	2.90	3.36	4.50	5.04
9	1.83	2.26	2.82	3.25	4.30	4.78
10	1.81	2.23	2.76	3.17	4.14	4.59
12	1.78	2.18	2.68	3.05	3.93	4.32
14	1.76	2.14	2.62	2.98	3.79	4.14
16	1.75	2.12	2.58	2.92	3.69	4.01
18	1.73	2.10	2.55	2.88	3.61	3.92
20	1.72	2.09	2.53	2.85	3.55	3.85
25	1.71	2.06	2.48	2.79	3.45	3.72
30	1.70	2.04	2.46	2.75	3.39	3.65
40	1.68	2.02	2.42	2.70	3.31	3.55
60	1.67	2.00	2.39	2.66	3.23	3.46
120	1.66	1.98	2.36	2.62	3.16	3.37
∞	1.64	1.96	2.33	2.58	3.09	3.29

Joint Matriculation Board

TABLE 3 : Critical values for the Wilcoxon signed-rank test

The table shows the critical values of T for a significance level of 5%.

n	two-tail test	one-tail test
5		0
6	0	2
7	2	3
8	3	5
9	5	8
10	8	10
11	10	13
12	13	17
13	17	21
14	21	25
15	25	30
16	29	35
17	34	41
18	40	47
19	46	53
20	52	60
21	58	67
22	65	75
23	73	83
24	81	91
25	89	100
26	98	110
27	107	119
28	116	130
29	126	140
30	137	151

Appendix

The line of best fit

To find the values of a and b which minimise $\sum_1^n \left(y_i - (a + bx_i) \right)^2$ it is convenient to work relative to the mean values $\bar{x}$ and $\bar{y}$. It is also convenient to consider the mean of the squared deviations.

$$\frac{1}{n} \sum_1^n \left(y_i - (a + bx_i) \right)^2 = \frac{1}{n} \sum_1^n \left((y_i - \bar{y}) - b(x_i - \bar{x}) + (\bar{y} - a - b\bar{x}) \right)^2$$

Expanding the RHS gives six terms

$$\frac{1}{n} \sum_1^n (y_i - \bar{y})^2 \quad = \text{Var}(Y)$$

$$\frac{1}{n} \sum_1^n b^2 (x_i - \bar{x})^2 \quad = \text{Var}(X)$$

$$\frac{1}{n} \sum_1^n (\bar{y} - a - b\bar{x})^2 = (\bar{y} - a - b\bar{x})^2$$

$$-\frac{2b}{n} \sum_1^n (y_i - \bar{y})(x_i - \bar{x}) \quad = -2b \, \text{Cov}(X, Y)$$

$$\frac{2}{n} \sum_1^n (y_i - \bar{y})(\bar{y} - a - b\bar{x}) = \frac{2}{n}(\bar{y} - a - b\bar{x}) \sum_1^n (y_i - \bar{y}) = 0$$

$$-\frac{2b}{n} \sum_1^n (x_i - \bar{x})(\bar{y} - a - b\bar{x}) = 0$$

It is therefore required to minimise

$$\text{Var}(Y) - 2b \, \text{Cov}(X, Y) + b^2 \, \text{Var}(X) + (\bar{y} - a - b\bar{x})^2$$

The parameter a appears only in the squared term and so must be chosen to make

$$\bar{y} - a - b\bar{x} = 0.$$

The regression line therefore passes through the point $(\bar{x}, \bar{y})$, as might have been expected.

The expression to be minimised is then a quadratic in b :

$$\text{Var}(Y) - 2b \, \text{Cov}(X, Y) + b^2 \, \text{Var}(X)$$

The quadratic is minimum when

$$b = \frac{\text{Cov}(X, Y)}{\text{Var}(X)}$$

Substituting this value for b, the mean of the squared deviations is then equal to

$$\text{Var}(Y) - \frac{\text{Cov}^2(X, Y)}{\text{Var}(X)} = \text{Var}(Y)(1 - r^2)$$

where r is the product moment correlation coefficient. From this expression, it can be seen that the line of best fit is good (i.e. the sum of squared deviations is small) when $r^2 \approx 1$ i.e. when $r \approx +1$ or $r \approx -1$.

> **The values of a and b which minimise the sum of squared deviations are denoted by $\hat{a}$ and $\hat{b}$.**
>
> $$\hat{b} = \frac{\text{Cov}(X, Y)}{\text{Var}(X)}$$
>
> $$\hat{a} = \bar{y} - \hat{b}\bar{x}$$

The expressions $\hat{a}$ and $\hat{b}$ are read as 'a hat' and 'b hat'.